Above, Down, Inside & Out

Unleashing Your Spiritual Giant Within

Michael J. Norman, B.S., D.C.

Abundance and Prosperity Center

Copyright © 2000

by
Michael J. Norman, B.S., D.C.

All rights reserved, including the right to reproduce this work in any form whatsoever, without permission in writing from the author, except for brief passages in connection with a review.

For information write:
Abundance & Prosperity Center
P.O. Box 116774
Carrollton, Texas 75011-6774

Cover Design & Artwork: Gary Tormos
Inside Design: Chesle H. Blair
Edited by: Keron Finnigan
Published by: Abundance & Prosperity Center
Carrollton, TX

Printed by:
Brown Books
Dallas

ISBN: 0-9676816-0-X
Library of Congress Catalog Card Number: 99-97286
2nd printing, revised

Table of Contents

Introduction

I. The History of a Profession — 5

   1. The Spinal Adjustment Is Not New!

   2. A Return To An Ancient Healthcare System

II. The Energy of Our Universe — 13

   1. Infinite Universal Energy

   2. Finite Man-Made Energy

III. Our Spiritual Nature Within — 23

   1. Amnesia at Birth

   2. Children as Teachers and Pupils

IV. Our Nervous System — 31

V. The Seven Areas of Life — 39

VI. If We Are Not Growing, We Are Dying — 55

   1. Growth Through Goal Setting

   2. The Twelve Steps to Goals of Abundance and Prosperity

   3. The Pain of Regret

VII. Alignment to Spirit Within-Lives of Abundance and Prosperity	69
VIII. Getting in the Way of Spirit Within-The Subluxated Nervous System	75
IX. The Physical Subluxation	79
1. Correction of the Physical Subluxation	
2. Law of Moderation	
X. The Mental Subluxation	85
1. Correction of the Mental Subluxation	
2. The Law of Giving and Receiving	
XI. Unleashing Your Spiritual Giant Within!	99

Dedication

To my wife, Laura. Thank you for just being you. A great person, a wonderful wife and the best mom a child could have.

To my daughter, Madison Elizabeth. Your entrance into this world was miraculous and you continue to be a miracle every day of our lives.

Acknowledgments

I am grateful for this opportunity to express my appreciation to the people who helped me in my growth, who have *patiently* supported me along the way, and who helped me make this book a reality.

I would first of all like to thank my parents, Joe and Kathleen, who have given me the gift of life and the freedom to develop it. Thank you for your support every step of the way. I love you both very much. To my wife, Laura, who has taught me to stand up for truth and principle, especially in the face of injustice; and to my daughter, Madison Elizabeth, who is one of those "old souls" who came here to teach the real importance in life; I love you both, and I continue to learn from you.

To Dee Morton, for her unceasing support and her greatest gift to me, her daughter, Laura Paige, my wife. To my brothers, John and Tim, for a wonderful childhood which I long to re-experience. You are my best friends and you inspire me to do better every day through your examples. To my late grandmother, Frances Veronica, who left me too early, but who continues to inspire me today through her tireless example of sacrifice and love. And to my late grandfather, Joe, who had a wonderful spirit, unlike any I will ever know again.

I want to express my gratitude to all my patients that I have had the privilege to adjust over the years. I thank you for allowing me to do what I love to do. You have taught me far more than I could ever repay. I also thank you for helping me get our message out to others about chiropractic, and the philosophy of above, down, inside and out.

I would like to thank the following people who assisted me in the preparation of this manuscript. This is my first book, and without you it would not have been possible. Dr. Robin Hyman, Kay Smith, Skip Olson, Barbara Olson, Mary Harris, Gary Tormos, Chance Parker and Parker Professional Products Inc. I appreciate all of you very much. And a special thanks to the late Dr. James Parker, who provided my initial foundation of universal law and chiropractic philosophy.

For all those who have loved and supported me along the way who, if mentioned in their entirety, would fill the pages of this book. You know who you are, and I love you very much.

May all of you be blessed with a rich increase of God's almighty good!

Introduction

"The true physician will be a teacher; his work will be to keep people well, instead of attempting to make them well after sickness and disease comes on; and still beyond this there will come a time when each will be his own physician.
.........the true teacher will never stand as the interpreter of truth for another. The true teacher is the one whose endeavor is to bring the one he teaches to a true knowledge of himself and hence of his own interior powers, that he may become his own interpreter.
  Ralph Waldo Trine from <u>In Tune With The Infinite</u>, 1899.

    This is a story about our spiritual selves, about tapping into the potential of who we are supposed to be, and about living life to the fullest. It is about realizing that we are living in a lavish universe of unlimited abundance and prosperity; however, we are the only ones who can get in the way and block it. This book is not only about returning the spirituality to healthcare, but about the terrible price we pay when we separate the two. It is about remembering that we are beings of spirit. Moreover, it is about the energy that runs our universe, how it actually permeates our bodies, running us. And finally, you will learn that the vehicle this energy uses to travel in our body is our nervous system. More important, you will learn that the direction in which the energy travels within us is from "above, down, inside and out."

Above, Down, Inside and Out. Although these appear to be four simple words, don't let appearances fool you. In short, these four words sum up the entire philosophy of chiropractic, a healthcare approach that inwardly transforms the body's physiology. A philosophy that is, unfortunately, not often enough conveyed to chiropractic patients, or to the general public at large. And, sad but true, many of today's "modern" chiropractic doctors are either forgetting, ignoring, or possibly have never even been taught this philosophy.

The following pages are an attempt to remedy this condition. This book could have easily extended into 400 pages but it was kept intentionally short. The idea for this book was initially an educational tool for the patients in my office, but I feel a greater need exists for what is in these pages. There is a need for the philosophy of chiropractic, or above, down, inside and out, (or ADIO), to reach out from the chiropractic office into the general public and beyond.

Today it is estimated that only 15% of the current U.S. population receives chiropractic care. This unfortunate low number can only be due to the failure of chiropractic to tell people what we do and why it works. Great strides and advancements in chiropractic have been made recently with the medical and scientific communities acknowledging chiropractic's effectiveness for pain relief and neck and low back injuries. However, you will immediately see that this is such an unbelievably small part of the chiropractic picture. To limit chiropractic to only pain relief is like limiting God to only Catholicism! We are merely scratching the surface.

The purpose of this book is to show what is possible for us

when we are maximally expressing the spirit of life. Whether this book found you as a current or prospective patient; a medical, chiropractic, osteopathic or other health professional; or just an individual who longs for greater knowledge on health and healing, this book is for you. This book is for everybody because it is about everybody. But keep in mind that, as you are reading, you may receive a faint feeling that you remember all of this from somewhere. You may feel like all the information somehow fits together and makes perfect sense. Don't worry if this occurs because the following pages of this book are not new to you. This book can only serve as a reminder. A reminder deep down to our spiritual selves which are longing to awake.

My greatest hope for this book is that it provides the reader the first step that is necessary for any transformation. The first step is a new conscious awareness leading to unlimited abundance and prosperity for the individual as they "rise above" the everyday physical world. By making this small but important first step today, we move closer to lifting our entire planet to a higher consciousness for tomorrow.

Notes

Chapter One
The History of a Profession

"Health requires an understanding of the nature of the universe and it's relationship to man."
                    Hippocrates, The Father of Medicine, 400 B.C.

In the year 1895, a Canadian from Port Perry, Ontario, named Daniel David Palmer, was a practicing magnetic healer in Davenport, Iowa. It was during this year that he decided to treat a janitor named Harvey Lillard, who had been deaf for 14 years. Palmer noticed that Lillard had a "bump" on his neck as he performed his examination. However, after concluding that Lillard's "bump" was a cervical vertebra that had become displaced, he decided to abandon the usual magnetic treatment in favor of a new procedure that he wanted to try.

After receiving his permission, Palmer placed Lillard on his treatment table and then, with his gentle hands, "adjusted" the vertebra back into position. Within a few days, two major events happened. Lillard's hearing was restored and Daniel David Palmer, (or D.D.), became the proud new founder and discoverer of a new profession. The new profession would be called chiropractic. Chiro comes from the Greek word, *cheir*, meaning "hand". Practic comes from the Greek, *praktikos*, a word for "effective practice". In other words, the term chiropractic stands for "effective use of the hands."

D. D. Palmer's young son, Bartlett Joshua, or B.J., became fascinated with this newly discovered science and became one of his father's best pupils, immersing himself in his studies. However, tension began to subtly develop between the two as B.J. believed that this new science should be taught to others, whereas D.D. wanted his discovery to remain a family secret. Although a huge family rift would later emerge, the science of chiropractic could not be stifled and began to catch the eyes of the masses.

D.D. eventually started a chiropractic school, but with little financial success. So, at age 18, B.J., took over the school and soon placed it on solid financial ground. He would continue to operate it successfully for the remainder of his life. B.J.'s career was a never-ending pursuit in his beloved chiropractic. B.J.'s life was one of incredible determination in the face of constant condemnation by the medical profession. His strength came from the conviction that chiropractic is consistent with the laws of the universe, and the universe interacts with us from above, down, inside and out.

By the time of his death in 1961, B. J. Palmer had literally educated enough doctors of chiropractic to place them throughout the free world. As of today, 103 years after chiropractic's discovery, the profession has grown into the second largest healing profession in the United States! Although technically still under the label in our society of "alternative" health care, the day is fast approaching when chiropractic's approach to healthcare will become our "mainstream" healthcare choice.

The only alternative healthcare will be our current, out-dated medical philosophy of health, which views our universe and our external environment as something that must be overcome, dominated, and conquered, instead of recognizing its awesome power and maximizing our connection to it.

For centuries, our society has mistakenly treated the mind, body, and spirit as separate entities. A portion of this mindset can be traced back to the 16th century, when many of the scientists of the day made a deal with the Catholic church to exclude the mind, emotions, and soul from scientific theories. Since this time, anyone who remotely attempted to intertwine healing with the spiritual was ostracized, incarcerated, or physically harmed by the "establishment." Under the guise of practicing medicine without a license, chiropractors were routinely thrown in jail as recently as the 1970's!

Even today, we unfortunately see this "separateness" trend continuing by our medical health care system of "specialists." But we are slowly seeing who is committing the true crimes in our society. It is absolute madness and absolute criminality to continue with our drug-based society, not to mention the medical tenet of treating one part of the body without believing you affect the whole. As true spiritual beings, every pill we take, whether it is prescribed, over-the-counter, or bought on a street corner, separates us from our true selves and prevents us from learning the truth of who we are. The longer these "specialists" keep treating our bodies as machines, failing to see beyond the physical, the more they are reinforcing the belief that we are helpless passengers in our own bodies.

This reminds me of a story told by the Buddha, regarding the natural tendency of human beings to steadfastly, or stubbornly, hold on to old and unsuccessful beliefs.

"A young widowed father had a five year old son whom he loved dearly. One day while he was away on business, robbers came into his village, looting and setting the village on fire and kidnapping his son. When he returned home he was extremely distraught and took the charred remains of another child to be his own. He provided an elaborate funeral service for the child and had him cremated, placing his ashes in a bag that he kept with him unceasingly.
One day the man's real son escaped from the robbers and came back to his father's new house. The son arrived in the middle of the night and knocked on his father's door, who continued to be very distraught over the loss of his son. As the son knocked and knocked he could hear his father crying inside. The father thought it was a cruel joke by someone who wanted to further torment him, and he angrily yelled for the boy to leave. The boy continued to knock and pleaded with his father to let him in, all to no avail. Finally, the boy left and the father and son never saw each other again."

After telling this story, the Buddha reportedly said: *"Sometime, somewhere you take some idea or belief to be the truth. If you cling to it too strongly, then when the truth comes in person to knock at your door, you will not open it."*

Unlike this story, the stubbornness of holding on to unsuccessful beliefs will never occur with chiropractic. Because times are changing, this trend of separateness and specialists is being slowly reversed with chiropractic leading the charge. Chiropractic, unlike many other health approaches, recognizes the whole person. The whole person includes the *entire* triad of the physical, mental, and the spiritual. The day is fast approaching in our health industry that, to address one aspect of the triad without the others, will be considered substandard care and will no longer be tolerated by our society. Chiropractic welcomes that day.

The Spinal "Adjustment" is Not New!

Although chiropractic has only been in existence since its discovery in 1895, the adjustment of the spine and its benefit to our nervous system are nothing new. The philosophy of above, down, inside and out is a universal truth that will never change as long as human beings live on this planet. And, like all great truths, the philosophy of above, down, inside and out, and the relationship of our nervous system to our lives were both talked about and practiced by some of our greatest thinkers and physicians as well as some of the oldest and greatest of our past civilizations.

From Hippocrates (the father of medicine), Galen (the prince of physicians), Alcmaeon of Croton (the father of Optholomology), to the 19th century bone-setters of the British Isles, many notable people in history have recognized the importance of the nervous system in relation to disease and pathology. The wisdom of the vertebral adjustment to free impaired nerves has stood the test of time and remained alive today after 5000 years. In fact, today's chiropractors are merely the present "guardians" of this ancient practice.

Archaeological studies have found significant documented proof of spinal adjusting procedures by ancient civilizations. Some of the older evidence indicating the prevalence of spinal adjusting procedures come from ancient and middle-age records, such as hieroglyphics, Greek papyrus records, and ancient Chinese documents. These have all indicated the use of various forms of spinal adjusting for the relief and treatment of numerous ailments. Chinese Kong Fu documents date back to

2700 B.C., while Greek records date back to 1500 B.C.

Some of the many civilizations and tribal groups who developed spinal adjusting skills include the early American Indians, the early natives of Polynesia, the Japanese, the Asiatic Indians, the Egyptians, the Babylonians, the Syrians, the Hindus, and the Tibetans. Research has also shown that other, more recent Indian tribes practiced spinal adjusting as well. These more recent tribes include the Sioux, the Winnebago, the Creek, the Aztec, the Toltec, the Tarascan, the Zoltec, the Mayan, and the South American Incas. With this type of crossover into different cultures, and communication between these cultures being almost zero, the spinal adjustment to improve the function of the human body proves to be an immutable universal truth!

Although condemnation from the medical "establishment" attempted to derail chiropractic after its 1895 discovery, records have shown that it may have started much earlier. Interestingly enough, spinal adjusting became so popular in the mid 1800's in England and the British Isles that the medical community complained about these "bone-setters." In the January 5, 1865 issue of the British Medical Journal, an article was published by Sir James Paget, complaining of the adverse economic impact these "bone-setters" were having on the medical profession!

A Return To An Ancient Healthcare System

The ancient Chinese had a wonderful system of healthcare. This system would be welcome today in our society by all chiropractors. In ancient China, doctors were only paid when their patients were well. The moment they got sick, the doctor stopped receiving any type of payment for his services. The doctor was viewed as not performing his job if his patient became ill. What a fascinating concept; to be paid according to your effectiveness and the type of results you get.

Although current emergency medicine procedures are tremendously effective, the remainder of today's medical health care industry should be called the "sick care industry." While it is becoming more and more expensive, our society is getting sicker and sicker. Could you imagine our doctors of today, only receiving payment if their patients were well? If this system were enacted, there would be an outrage unlike anything we have ever seen. If this "payment for wellness" plan ever went into effect, our doctors of today, would be on the welfare rolls. And that is only if they didn't abandon the industry altogether.

However, not all doctors would suffer in this system of healthcare. Chiropractic would welcome this system of healthcare upon our planet and would be the top-wage earners in healthcare. Chiropractors have always been and will always be "wellness doctors." The majority of individuals do not come to chiropractors because they are sick. They come to chiropractors because they have a desire to stay well.

This desire to stay well comes from the understanding of the philosophy of remaining "in tune" with the spirit of our incredibly lavish and abundant universe. With chiropractic's help in removing subluxations, this incredibly lavish and abundant spirit is maximally expressed within each of us as it travels above, down, inside and out.

This "payment for wellness" plan of healthcare may not be as far-fetched as it sounds. It is my belief, as a physician, the doctor of the future will break free of today's traditional fee-for-service method of healthcare. The doctor will become a "lifestyle consultant," assisting and empowering individuals in all aspects of life (see seven areas of life in chapter five).

The doctor will be compensated only by the results the individuals attain. Similar to a tithe within our religious institutions of today, the doctor of the future will receive compensation from a portion of the *"fruits of increase"* an individual begins to manifest in his life since beginning work with the doctor. By fruits of increase I am referring to prosperity that can come in many forms. In fact, it is my belief that this compensation method will become commonplace throughout our planet as we all move ever closer to a spiritual economy.

Let us now begin to explore the power of chiropractic by first discussing the workings of our universe.

Chapter Two
The Energy Of Our Universe

"There is no such thing as disorder. Only orders of indefinitely high degree."
David Bohm, University of London physicist

Some people have the mistaken notion that our universe and planet were created by some "cosmic car wreck." That is, the old Newtonian idea where every thing was formed by chance, with no rhyme or reason for its creation, and thus no purpose. This is a grave miscalculation on their part, for an individual who thinks in this manner currently trods through life with a mindset that I would not wish upon my worst enemy. This mindset can be illustrated by the example of the dog and the flea. In other words, think of our universe as one giant dog and a human being as a tiny flea on the dog's tail. To even remotely think that we as a tiny flea are "wagging" the dog instead of the dog wagging us is utter foolishness.

But this is the mindset many individuals possess by taking

our universe for granted and by thinking that the human being is the only controlling element in our universe. We see this commonly within the scientific community when scientists think they have discovered or created what God has afforded them the privilege to discover or create. In their smallness and foolishness, they use their discoveries and creations as reasons to question the very existence of the one who gave them their ability to think in the first place. These individuals are like fish swimming up the river, totally unaware of the water around them. They only become aware of the water and the absolute complexity of their universe after winding up on the hook of a fisherman and being pulled out of the water. And then it is too late.

We live in the midst of an incredibly lavish and incredibly abundant universe. It is a universe that is so vast that it is beyond human comprehension. In Michael Talbot's fascinating book, The Holographic Universe, he states that our universe, despite its apparent materiality and enormous size, does not exist in and of itself, but is the "stepchild" of something far vaster and more ineffable. He goes on to state that there is every reason to believe there are limitless further universes beyond ours, all existing in infinitely increasing stages of further development! In other words, there is no end to the universe.

Throughout this vastness of our universe, there is an absolute intelligent order that exists. Every aspect of our universe has an absolute purpose to justify its existence. However, many of these purposes currently reside beyond our human comprehension. This intelligent order is run by an all-pervading energy that encompasses and controls everything, from the movements of our planets, and the tides of our oceans, to the changing of the seasons and even the activities of the human body. This energy is the foundation that has given birth to everything in our universe and contains every subatomic particle that has ever been or ever will be.

Amazingly, as Michael Talbot states in his book, when physicists have tried to calculate the minimum amount of energy in our universe, they find that every cubic centimeter of empty space contains more energy than the total energy of all the matter in the known universe! That means one centimeter of space in our universe could contain the energy of a trillion atomic bombs. This amount of energy, however, requires an understanding that human comprehension is not quite ready to hold at this time.

Although millions of us attribute this energy to be the spirit of God, we are now routinely seeing even the past skeptical scientific community acknowledging some type of "infinite intelligence" that governs our cosmos. To look at our universe any other way would be shallow and foolish. To me, what says it all, is what the master of the scientific community, Albert Einstein, concluded after a career of studying this universal energy. Einstein's entire life's work was meant to show that all perceived hard matter, including human beings, is mainly empty space with this universal energy running through it. Absolutely convinced of an all intelligent God running the universe and seeing the smallness of science, his viewpoint took on a spiritual tone as he remarked, *"I want to know God's thoughts……the rest are details."*

Every living entity in our universe has this same energy. Every plant, animal, tree, insect, bird, etc. has the energy coursing through them, allowing them to function. As human beings we are no different. We have this abundant and limitless energy traveling through us. This energy allows our hearts to beat, digests our meals, sends white blood cells to our organs, conceives a child, listens to music, and countless millions of other functions all at the exact same moment. Could you imagine waking up in the morning and trying to remember to do all these functions?

Deepak Chopra, a true pioneer in mind-body medicine, makes an interesting point regarding the interconnectedness of this energy through our breathing. With each breath we take in and let out 10^{22} atoms. This means we are inhaling and exhaling countless atoms every day that have been in the bodies of countless other human beings going back to the beginning of time. These same atoms have also been inside trees, animals, plants, and every other type of matter in our universe. Additionally, as I study quantum physics, I am of the opinion that these are also the same atoms that will encompass all things that will exist in our universe's future, all the way to the end of time. We cannot deny our interconnectedness.

We have two options when it comes to this powerful energy that commands our universe. We can either align with it, allowing our lives to flow perfectly and effortlessly, or we can resist it, blocking it through actions and consciousness of our own making. The energy of our universe will always be there, awaiting our decision. Nevertheless, it is *our* decision to make.

Everything in the universe contains energy. But we can categorize this energy into two distinctly different types. It is now necessary to discuss the two different types of energy that we should never allow to get confused.

Infinite Universal Energy

The first type of energy is what we have just been discussing. It is the infinite energy of the universe that pervades all things and maintains the absolutely purposeful and intelligent order of all things. This type of energy is inexhaustible, never running out, and it is always available to us, just awaiting our decision to align with it. When we align with this type of energy, our lives begin to flow perfectly and effortlessly.

It is the attunement to the infinite universal energy that allows us to experience what I call, lives of unlimited "abundance and prosperity." This is how the great poets have written their poetry, how the great artists have constructed their masterpieces. This is how some of our enlightened spiritual masters have transcended the physical limits of their bodies with no need for sleep, food, drink or other physical necessities. In my opinion, this energy connection is how many of our spontaneous remissions from disease have occurred. It is as if a connection to an invisible, inexhaustible power source has been made, opening us up to the infinite supply of ideas, creations, discoveries, etc., that the universe decided it was time to introduce into our physical existence.

It takes absolutely no effort or struggle to generate or maintain this type of energy. In fact, this energy generates only feelings of peace and love when we are attuned to it. Aligning with infinite universal energy is what is commonly referred to as opening, listening, and following your heart. A wise teacher of mine was correct when he said, *"The heart shall guide you truly."*

When we open and follow our heart and align it to infinite universal energy, we experience an all encompassing peaceful and loving state that pervades our bodies. This is also accompanied by an incredible feeling of fulfillment within ourselves. This is important to remember within our lives, especially when we are facing a decision on a particularly difficult life path. We have all agonized at some point in our lives when we are forced to make a critical decision that has the potential of leading our lives in a totally different direction. However, by keeping the understanding of infinite universal energy in mind and knowing what it feels like, we are always guided to the right decision and the higher path. Always remember, when we move in the direction of internal peace, we are aligning with infinite energy. By consistently moving our lives in the direction of peace and choosing an ever increasing higher path for ourselves, we come into a total alignment with the infinite energy and move closer to lives of unlimited abundance and prosperity.

Another way to explain this energy is through vibration. Everything in the universe vibrates at a particular frequency. Heavier and denser objects vibrate at a lower frequency than lighter, smaller objects, which vibrate at higher frequencies. As human beings we are no different, although our frequencies vibrate according to our energy levels. When we are in tune with the infinite energy of the universe, we are vibrating at a higher frequency. When we are generating our own finite man-made energy, which we will discuss next, we drop to a lower vibration. As human beings, when our frequencies become too low, we begin to experience chaos in our lives. This chaos may appear in the form of illnesses, poverty, physical deterioration, depression, hopelessness, unexplained accidents, and many other such adverse conditions.

There is an ideal frequency level that every human being best resonates at. Every person has their own individual threshold. When vibration falls below this threshold, they experience the chaotic state mentioned above. But when vibration exceeds this threshold, not only do miracles occur, but a state of abundance and prosperity is attained. This is how we become enlightened individuals. The universe uses us to bring forth the great works, creations, or discoveries which the universe wants introduced into our physical world at this time.

Once we have experienced this state, even if only for an instant, this higher level of vibration becomes easier and easier to attain as we evolve our consciousness and continue to attune to the infinite energy of the universe.

The vibration of all matter is projected out of itself and vibrates throughout our entire universe. This vibration not only includes physical matter, but also includes thoughts and feelings that we possess. This is extremely important to note because this projection of vibration has an impact upon everything in our universe. The composite of all our vibrations determines the overall quality of life on our planet. In other words, this means that every thought, action, or deed since the beginning of time that has ever occurred (and possibly all that is to ever come in the future), is eternally contained and floating around within the infinite energy of our universe! Our current "contribution" to this vibrational melting pot impacts positively or negatively on the current state of our planet.

Although at first this appears to be a grave responsibilty for each of us, it is actually a tremendous opportunity to positively impact world consciousness. The synthesis of this infinite energy is love. By our willingness to feel love, for ourselves and others, we are brought into alignment with it. As an individual begins to align with infinite universal energy and their lives become more peaceful and loving, their vibrational level increases and other individuals begin to pick up on this. By raising our individual vibration levels, we act as comfort and support to others as they become encouraged to raise their vibration levels and move into more peaceful and loving states. As this activity continues, this higher consciousness will spread throughout our planet. This is how true change will occur, and it just takes a few individuals to get it started.

Finite Man-Made Energy

Now the second type of energy is drastically different. This is what I call finite man-made energy. It requires tremendous effort on our part to generate and is a constant struggle to maintain. This man-made energy is in limited supply, continually running out, forcing us to constantly seek out more and more of it. Finite man-made energy is totally at the mercy of our physical existence. As our bodies need food, sleep, drink, etc., this energy quickly dissipates. This energy keeps an individual at a very low vibrational level, leading us on an effortful, ceaseless, and dead-end pursuit as we attempt to fill an insatiable void within us. It feels like we are trying to swim against a strong current of a mighty river every day.

When we live from finite man-made energy we are never at peace within. To live in this way is what is commonly referred to as listening to the head instead of the heart. In fact, we are struggling with inner lives of chaos and turmoil. A life of pursuing this type of energy puts an individual in a state of "dis-ease" in all areas of life. This "dis-ease" state within our bodies is what soon will result in illness, depression, fatigue, accidents, poverty, relationship difficulties, and many other unpleasant physical manifestations.

We far too often rely more on our finite, self-generated energy instead of becoming in tune with the spirit of the infinite universal energy. We are often times fearful to relinquish control of our lives to the universe and we try to force the situations and circumstances of our lives. We feel the need to rely often on this finite energy because we forget who we are and where we come from. We forget that we are spiritual beings who are temporarily experiencing this physical and mental realm and there is definitely a better way of doing things without the effort and struggle of swimming against the current. When we force finite energy into our lives, we leave the universe no other choice but to show us the *absurbness* of this battle. We lose the battle by creating the chaos in our lives that we mentioned earlier.

However, this losing battle is part of the absolutely perfect order of our universe. The universe hopes we will eventually tire of constantly seeking out more of this finite man-made energy and will ultimately align with its perfect infinite energy. Although as human beings we are always given free choice, we are also always given guidance to follow a higher path as well. The higher path of aligning with the infinite energy of the universe brings us lives of abundance and prosperity and transcends us into who and what we were truly meant to be.

Chiropractic fully understands this infinite energy that governs our universe and everything living within it. This understanding forms the foundation of chiropractic's philosophy. A philosophy of working alongside the natural laws of our universe and maximizing our connection to the universe, which has been the purpose of chiropractic from the beginning. Next, as we talk briefly about who we really are as human beings, we will begin to see the philosophy of ADIO slowly come into focus.

Notes

Chapter Three
Our Spiritual Nature Within

"Only human beings have come to the point where they no longer know why they exist. They don't use their brains and they have forgotten the secret knowledge of their bodies, their senses or their dreams. They don't use the knowledge the spirit has put into every one of them; they are not even aware of this, and so they stumble along blindly on the road to nowhere-a paved highway which they themselves bulldoze and make smooth so that they can get faster to the big empty hole which they'll find at the end, waiting to swallow them up. It's a quick comfortable superhighway, but I know where it leads to. I've seen it. I've been there in my vision and it makes me shudder to think about it."
The Lakota shaman Lame Deer from
<u>Lame Deer Seeker of Visions</u>

Humanity and the world today get in trouble when they deny the "interconnectedness" of an all pervading energy of our universe. This fragmented way of thinking creates a fragmented world. We mistakenly think that we can extract valuable parts of the earth without affecting the whole, or we think we can separately address societal problems, like crime, drugs, poverty, etc., without addressing society as a whole. Furthermore, in the world of health, today's medical health "specialists" believe it is possible to treat one part of the body without affecting the whole. Amazingly, and I must agree, it has been hypothesized that if we continue this current trend of fragmentation, not only will our world continue to suffer, but it could ultimately lead to our extinction as a species!

We have to be careful not to mix up who we really are as human beings. The temptation and ease with which we forget are tremendous in our present day society; we sometimes have to stop and remind ourselves. We ARE the infinite energy of the universe that we have just discussed in the last chapter. As human beings we are actually "subsets" of the entire vastness of energy that runs our universe. In other words, the entire makeup and intelligence of every solar system within our universe resides within each of us! This includes every aspect of the universe that ever was and every aspect that will ever be. It's all one big connection. Try that on for size!

The energy of the universe is not some separate or distinct force that interacts with our physical bodies from time to time to make our lives easier, as many of us would like to believe. It is the other way around. Unfortunately, many times we are falsely taught that we exist equally as spiritual, mental and physical beings. This cannot be further from the truth. We are energy beings, or, in other words, spiritual beings temporarily experiencing a physical and mental existence. Our spiritual beings were here long before our physical and mental bodies were formed, and our spiritual beings will remain here long after the physical and mental bodies pass away. From spirit we came and to spirit we shall go.

Think of this whole process in terms of taking a vacation along the Atlantic Ocean. Imagine taking a drop of water out of the ocean and putting it into a test tube and sealing it up. The drop of water in the test tube is now a physically self-contained "subset" of the vast intelligence of the entire Atlantic Ocean. This "subset" of ocean water essentially is the entire Atlantic Ocean, containing all of its properties , only on a much smaller scale. Although that drop of water while in the ocean was infinitely intelligent and powerful, when it is contained in the test tube, it is subject to the limitations of the physical test tube. The test tube is able to temporarily direct and control the drop of once powerful ocean water.

Our bodies act in the same manner as the test tube! We are beings of spirit that originated from an infinitely intelligent and powerful universe that are now subject to the temporary limitations of our physical and mental bodies. This leaves two choices for the physical and mental aspects of our being. They can either allow the spiritual to flow freely and create lives of what I call "abundance and prosperity," or they can block or "subluxate" the spiritual essence of ourselves, creating lives of dis-ease, chaos, lack and limitation. These physical and mental subluxations lie at the heart of chiropractic's objective and philosophy. Now, with this said, the question becomes, "Why were we made with no conscious awareness of our spiritual essence within?"

Amnesia at Birth

I want to tell you a secret. Everything I am talking about in this book you already know, although you may not remember. Part of our purpose here on the planet is to remember who we are and how the Creator taught us to function in the universe. For many individuals, this realization comes too late, or not at all, resulting in much pain of regret that haunts them to the last day of their lives.

Many people ask me why God created a species like ourselves that is so perceptively lacking. The answer is simply because we asked Him to. This is His gift to us. Our job is to find our way back to Him and to remember who we really are. We are a spiritual being, projected into materiality to experience, to create, and to learn. This refines our soul, enabling us to find our way back to spirit and Him! The only catch to experiencing this materiality is that we have to check our memory at the door! Could you imagine trying to motivate yourself for life on earth, knowing full well the perfection you had just come from? I hardly think so. As you embrace the laws of the universe, you will discover that this amnesia is part of the perfection.

I think the idea of our spiritual amnesia is symbolically referred to in the Genesis story of Adam and Eve's expulsion from the garden of Eden. Think of Eden as a garden of unlimited abundance and prosperity that was initially given to all human beings. Because of their disobedience, Adam and Eve were in essence prevented from experiencing Eden. It was left up to them to find their way back. This search continues to this day. Our basic desire is to rediscover or return to our Eden.

As you could guess (just like everything else), our amnesia worsens with age. Believe it or not, as we enter our world as infants we remember who we truly are and the beautiful place we just came from. That's probably why we come kicking, screaming, and crying every step of the way! Jesus tells us: *"Let the children come to me, for the kingdom of God belongs to such as these. Amen, I say to you, whoever does not accept the kingdom of God like a child will not enter it"* (Mark 10:14-15). Because we live in a society that conditions us to "grow up," it is up to us to find our way back to that faithful and unconditional loving state that we all knew as children. Children are the best examples of what it is to be connected to the spirit within; therefore, they come not only as pupils, but also as our greatest teachers.

Children As Teachers and Pupils

One of my favorite stories about how our society conditions our wisdom at an early age, and ultimately covers up our spiritual essence, is told by author Noah benShea.

"Imagine a boy, sitting on a hill, looking out through his innocence on the beauty of the world. Slowly the child begins to learn. He does this by collecting small stones of knowledge, placing one on top of the other. Over time his learning becomes a wall he has built in front of himself. Now when he looks out, he can see his learning, but he has lost his view. This makes the man, who was once a boy, both proud and sad. The man, looking at his predicament, decides to take down the wall. But to take down a wall also takes time, and when he accomplishes this task, he has become an old man. The old man rests on the hill and looks out through his experience on the beauty of the world. He understands what has happened to him. He understands what he sees. But, he does not see, and will never see the world again, the way he saw it as a child on that first, clear morning."

This is a story about every one of us. Waking up to our true spiritual nature requires an awareness of this societal conditioning before we begin to remember who we really are. The greatest help through this process occurs if we allow children to teach us.

We seem to have the whole process backwards. Our society places importance in going out into the workplace to make our livings, while our children become a generation raised in daycare centers. This is a time we should be home with them, learning everything we can from them. Because this new life has just arrived from the spiritual realm, their memories are still fresh. This spiritual realm, which has long since been forgotten by us, is our purpose here on the planet. One of the easiest ways to relearn and recapture it is through the teachings of a child who has just recently arrived from the spiritual existence. In my opinion, these lessons that show us our own spiritual essence are worth selling everything we own to make it possible to be at home with our children at this time.

This time could also be spent teaching our children in such a way that society would not be successful in separating them from their spiritual essence later on. Could you imagine a society that valued this concept as a whole and reinforced the spiritual essence of human beings from the time of birth? Imagine at the time of birth, you were lucky enough to be taught that you just came from spirit and you have now come into materiality temporarily, to learn lessons, to understand your divine purpose, and to perfect yourself. Imagine you were taught that everything in the universe is in abundant supply, and you could have as much as you desire, and materiality had absolutely no power over you, except the power you give it or allow it. Imagine you were told all this was yours by only following a few simple universal laws that were taught to you as prevalently as the ABC's. Could you imagine the mistakes and grief this would save us in our lifetimes, and the incredible heights we could soar to and accomplish, without needing an entire lifetime of trial and error to do it?

Our job as parents is to begin making this scenario a reality with the next generation. By so doing, we will rediscover our spiritual selves in the process through the lessons our children have for us. If this were to become commonplace in our society, the spiritual evolution of our planet would advance at a speed never before experienced.

We shall now progress into a discussion of specifically where and how the energy and spirit of the universe flows through us as individuals. The philosophy of Above, Down, Inside and Out will come into even clearer focus now.

Notes

Chapter Four
Our Nervous System

"Do you not know that you are the temple of God, and that the spirit of God dwells in you?"
                                                    1 Corinthians 3:16

    During only the third week of fetal development, the first signs of a developing nervous system can already be observed in the baby. The nervous system, which consists of the brain and spinal cord, begins to form several weeks before any other organ or system in the body. There is clearly a reason for this early arrival. The nervous system is the absolute, master control system for the entire body. No other function of the body could occur unless it received the command from the nervous system. Figure 4.1 and 4.2 on the following pages illustrate this fact.

    However, there is one other important aspect of the nervous system. It is the place in us where this infinite energy of the universe that we have previously discussed in chapter two,

SPINAL NERVE DISTRIBUTION

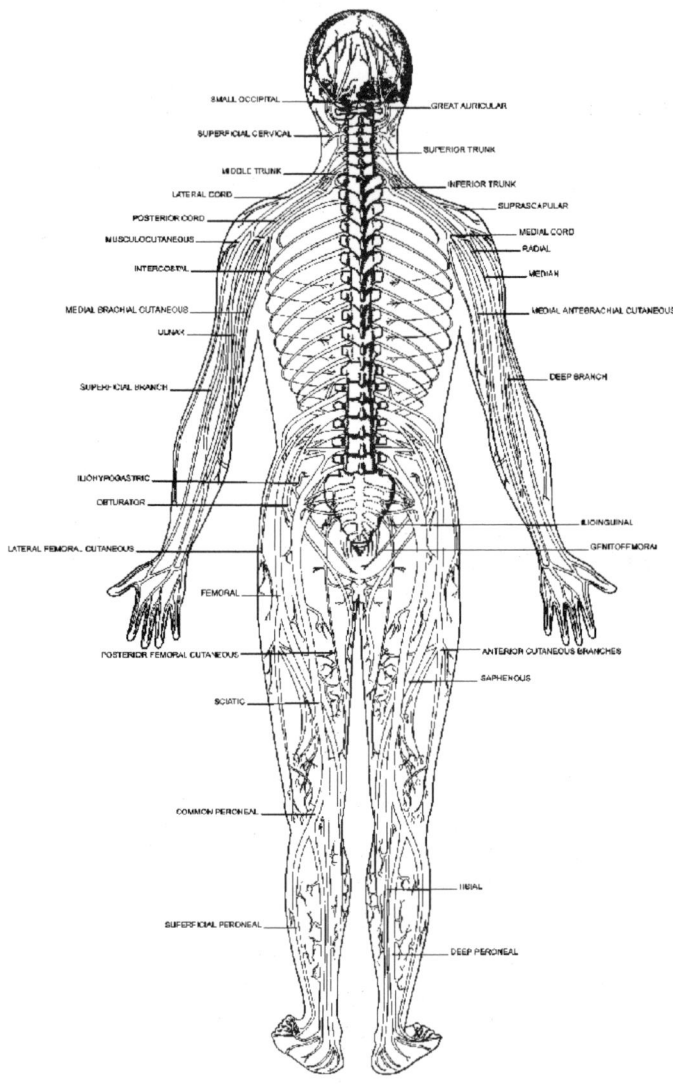

FIGURE 4.1

©1999 Parker Professional Products, Inc.

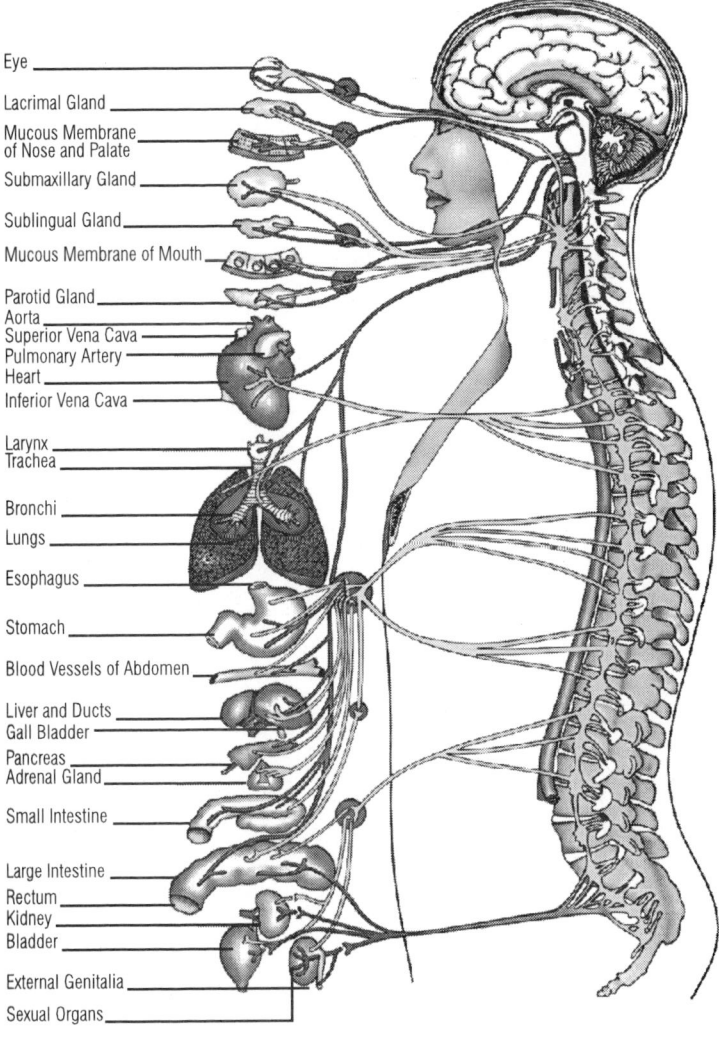

FIGURE 4.2

©1999 Parker Professional Products, Inc.

resides. In other words, the entire makeup and intelligence of our universe resides within each of us, using the nervous system as its means of transit! Hereafter we shall refer to the universe within as simply the spirit within.

Chiropractors are doctors of the nervous system for this very reason. This is where the philosophy of Above, Down, Inside and Out becomes very apparent. The identically same spirit that runs our universe and everything in it, operates within us via our nervous systems. Above, Down, Inside and Out is simply the philosophy of how this spirit flows and interacts between our universe and each of our individual nervous systems (see figure 4.3).

> **ABOVE:** The spirit of the universe comes down from above as it enters each individual through the brain or mental plane of existence.
>
> **DOWN:** The spirit then radiates downward from the mental plane into the spinal cord.
>
> **INSIDE:** The spirit then continues downward, permeating the entire length of the spinal cord.
>
> **OUT:** The spirit then radiates outward from the spinal cord throughout the network of nerves and travels throughout the entire body. Spirit then continues outward even more as it radiates from our bodies into our external environment as we interact and express ourselves to the people, places, and circumstances in each of our lives.

As we can see from Figure 4.3, we begin to align with the spirit of the universe by gaining an understanding of how it permeates us as individuals. The chiropractic philosophy of ADIO teaches individuals about the flow and direction of our interaction with universal spirit. With this in mind, we are

PRINCIPLE OF ABOVE, DOWN, INSIDE AND OUT

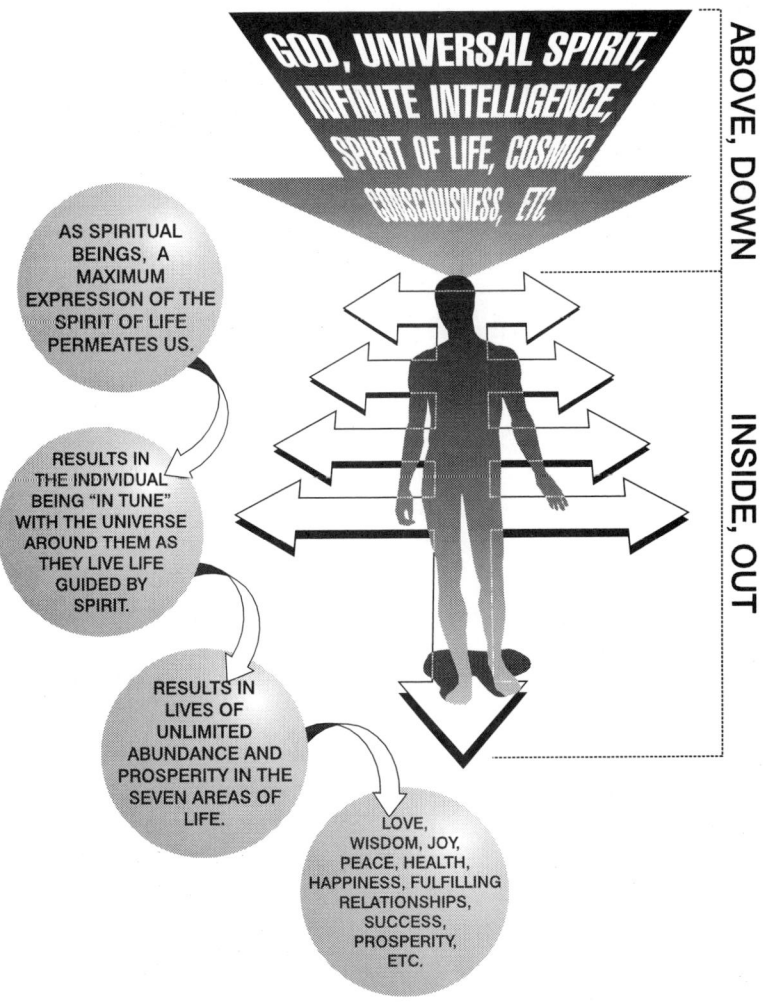

FIGURE 4.3

then able to prioritize areas of the human body and evaluate those areas for any interferences in the flow of spirit.

This is chiropractic. Chiropractors are doctors of our nervous system who remove interferences to the flow of spirit within us. Chiropractic is not about the pain in the shoulder, the sprained back, or the pulled muscle. Although this is a part of the chiropractic picture, it is an extremely tiny part. When the individual has a free flow of the spirit of the universe within the nervous system, the body heals itself, and these symptoms fade away.

This is ADIO, and chiropractic's objective is to maximize the expression of this spirit within an individual's nervous system. Think of the spirit of the universe flowing into us from above, down, inside and out, like a garden hose inserted through a hole in the top of our heads. Now visualize as the water is turned on, it comes down from above and enters into our head. The water is then directed down through the spinal cord and throughout the body via the thousands of nerves that exit the spinal cord. Then visualize the water projecting out from the body itself like our skin is springing leaks. Now imagine the nozzle of the hose being turned all the way up, creating a gush of water. This would be an example of maximum expression of the universe's spirit in that individual's nervous system.

After hearing this, it sounds as if we should never have a single problem or illness if we have the perfection of the universe running through us. And it certainly makes you wonder why you need a chiropractor to tamper with the perfection of the universe. But we as human beings can "block", or subluxate, the maximum expression of this spirit within our nervous systems. These subluxations occur on an individual's physical and mental planes of existence, affecting our spiritual health within. Herein lies the purpose of a chiropractor: to evaluate and remove from the nervous system these physical and mental subluxations that lessen the expression of the spirit within.

Step one of this process begins with a look at just how an individual's life is currently existing in the physical plane of existence. This is accomplished by evaluating what is called an individual's "seven areas of life." The seven areas of life include the physical, financial, social, family, mental, career, and spiritual components which constitute one's life. When physical and mental subluxations exist, thereby blocking our spiritual nature, our lives are affected adversely in these seven distinct areas. *When it comes to evaluation of the expression of spirit within our nervous systems, there is no greater barometer or measuring stick than how we are faring in these seven areas.*

Notes

Chapter Five
The 7 Areas of Life

"If gravity is the glue that holds the universe together, balance is the key that unlocks it's secrets. Balance applies to our body, mind, and emotions, to all levels of our being. It reminds us that anything we do, we can overdo or underdo, and that if the pendulum of our lives or habits swings too far to one side, it will inevitably swing to the other."
Dan Millman from <u>The Laws of Spirit.</u>

Throughout this book you will hear about the "seven areas of life." When we talk of the physical and mental planes of existence, there are seven areas that all human beings experience in one form or the other. These are seven different but totally equal areas, with no one area any more or any less important than the others. When we are guided by a maximum expression of our spirit, with no subluxations present, these seven areas of life flow perfectly and effortlessly. The result of this is what we refer to as living in a state of abundance and prosperity consciousness. Although we will discuss abundance and prosperity in the next chapter, it is a state that results from growing and integrating all of the seven areas of life within our existence. It is truly a powerful state to live in.

However, these seven areas are also the areas of suffering in human beings, when the presence of physical or mental subluxations exists. As the subluxation blocks the spirit of the universe as it attempts to permeate us from above, down, inside and out, we become "un-attuned" with the universe around us. This condition manifests in numerous forms of chaos and imbalance in the seven areas of our physical existence. Manifestations might include conditions such as physical illness, poverty, pain syndromes, relationship difficulties, loss of imagination, depression, unemployment or a host of many others.

Figure 5.1 illustrates this fact by showing how we are truly spiritual beings temporarily experiencing the physical and mental planes of existence. As you can see, the seven areas of life are just ""subsets" within the temporary physical and mental planes. The choice is entirely ours to make, by either allowing these seven areas to flow perfectly, creating lives of abundance and prosperity, or we can experience these seven areas as lives of dis-ease, chaos, limitation and lack, through physical and mental subluxations.

The following is a brief rundown of the seven areas of life in our physical and mental existence. They include a brief description and a few activities that are helpful for growth in that particular area of life. Examples of difficulties of each area due to the presence of subluxations are also included.

1. Physical

The physical area of life includes the overall physical well

THE 7 AREAS OF LIFE

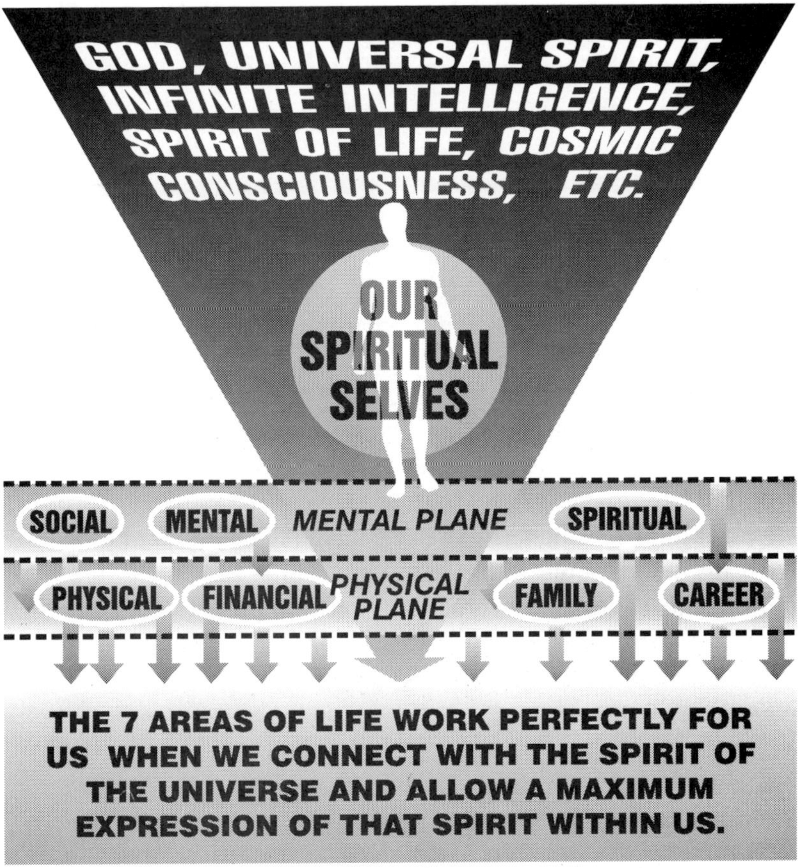

GOD, UNIVERSAL SPIRIT, INFINITE INTELLIGENCE, SPIRIT OF LIFE, COSMIC CONSCIOUSNESS, ETC.

OUR SPIRITUAL SELVES

SOCIAL • MENTAL • *MENTAL PLANE* • SPIRITUAL

PHYSICAL • FINANCIAL • *PHYSICAL PLANE* • FAMILY • CAREER

THE 7 AREAS OF LIFE WORK PERFECTLY FOR US WHEN WE CONNECT WITH THE SPIRIT OF THE UNIVERSE AND ALLOW A MAXIMUM EXPRESSION OF THAT SPIRIT WITHIN US.

FIGURE 5.1

being of the body. Growth in this area can be achieved by regular exercise, regular doctor check-ups, proper nutrition, a pleasant appearance, proper body weight, etc. Physical and mental subluxations in this area of life may manifest as illness, pain syndromes, fatigue, improper body weight, improper or unpleasant physical appearance, loss of strength or vitality and many others. We will not go into great detail with the physical area of life due to it being sufficiently covered in other areas of the book.

2. Financial

The financial area of life usually gets the majority of our attention, but keep in mind it is an area equal to the other six. By consistently devoting more attention to any one area, we create an imbalance that can eventually manifest into a physical condition as well as causing all seven areas to suffer. Growth in the financial area would include proper budget and expenses, proper investments and savings, proper earnings, proper credit card usage, proper insurance, estate planning, wills, etc. Physical and mental subluxations in this area of life may manifest as insufficient financial income or poverty, improper debt accumulation, irresponsibility in estate planning with regard to insurance, wills, etc., a failure to pay yourself first, a constant creation of unexpected expenses and many others.

It is important to note that the reason the financial area receives so much of our attention, is we have made money the ultimate symbol of power in our physical world. By doing this, we pay a substantial price. This empowerment of money is in violation of universal law and many underlying conditions manifest in this area of life for this very reason. When we empower anything external to us, money or otherwise, we automatically dis-empower or de-value ourselves. As we look around our society today, we need not look far before we find an individual struggling with issues in the financial area of life.

The universe knows how to get our attention and uses our greatest physical symbol of power to do it. One example of this can be seen prevalently in today's society with the out-of-control debt which individuals are ringing up. Debt is a symptom, not the problem. In my opinion, debt is a socially acceptable way of punishing ourselves and results from a refusal to forgive ourselves. This self-punishment can be the result of events and circumstances which occurred to us many years ago and we unforgivingly refuse to let them go. These underlying events and circumstances are many times missed because we see only debt as the problem. Therefore, the true cause of the problem is never addressed and the symptom runs wildly out of control.

It is my belief that there will come a time in our evolution that money will disappear from our planet. The world will sever its attachment to it and the power we have put into money will dissipate, thus rendering it irrelevant. Money will return to its original purpose, which is to serve only as a convenient method of exchange for a particular item or service rendered. When this occurs, our planet will be one in which the spirit and soul of a human being will be raised up and valued as the true asset, and money will again assume its rightful purpose as merely a "useful tool."

3. Social

The social area of life is our connection to others on our planet. We can not live without it. Growth in this area includes support groups, community activities, friendships, gaining the respect of others, proper manners, caring and compassion, sense of humor, listening skills, self confidence, etc.

Physical and mental subluxations in this area of life may manifest as loneliness, excessive introversion or extroversion, poor self image/self confidence, depression, a feeling of separateness from others, an inability or refusal to connect with others, unhappiness, no sense of humor, lack of compassion or caring, sociopathic tendencies and many others.

Numerous studies have shown not only the benefit, but the absolute necessity of consistently being in the company of others. Physical health improves tremendously when one is consistently in the company of others, compared to individuals who choose to avoid social interaction. In fact, one of our primary purposes on this planet is to develop our connection to other human beings. Jesus tells us, *"You shall love your neighbor as yourself."* (Mark 12:31).

However, we must not wait on our society to support us and encourage us to seek out the company of our neighbors and love them as we love ourselves. We must remember that we currently live in a society that has taught us that happiness finally will be ours when we can separate ourselves from the rest of society. We are told, happiness will occur when we can move away from the crowded, noisy, people-filled city and into the "promised land." The promised land in this case may be a nearby suburb with a high-security, gated community, waiting for us with a 24-hour security guard stationed at the entrance to keep the "undesirables" out. When we arrive, a house is waiting for us that is set far off the road with a long driveway attached to it. It contains the newest state-of-the-art security system, with an iron gate and fence surrounding the property. Although the house is already contained within a gated community, these other elements of "success" are to keep away the other people that are fortunate enough to be living within the high security, gated community with us. Now that we have finally achieved success and separated ourselves from the remainder of our society, it is now time to rest and enjoy our "success." However, upon looking around, there is no one with whom to share it.

I compare this to the story of the man who reached success by climbing a mountain all by himself. Loneliness forced him to jump off. Without a connection to others on our planet, we fail to realize one of the primary purposes in our lives.

4. Family

Although in reality we are all a family from the spirit of the universe, this area of life involves our genetic family into which we were born or raised. Growth in this area should include time spent with family, family vacations, family activities, listening skills, love, respect, support, forgiveness, becoming a good role model, consistent personal growth of all family members, etc. Physical and mental subluxations in this area of life may manifest as resentment, lack of respect, chaotic lifestyles that diminish time spent with family, stifled growth of any family member, lack of intimacy, addictive and habitual actions, insecurities, jealousies and numerous others.

Any time we discuss the family area of life it is extremely important to note that a majority of problems within a family are the result of subtle internal power struggles between family members that they may or may not be aware of. These power struggles are how each family member personally asserts their power and gains energy from their particular family dynamic. These power struggles are very damaging to the persons within the family and waste valuable energy that should be used for personal growth through unconditional love and support for the family unit. There are certain families that repeat this endless power struggle generation after generation. This leads family members to experience stifled personal growth and a consistent failure to live up to their full potentials. They are too wrapped up in the game of the subtle power struggles.

Within every family dynamic, there are four distinct personality classifications. Author James Redfield in his book entitled, The Celestine Prophecy, explains in great detail the relationship between these four classifications. A brief introduction to these classifications is outlined below. Although sometimes entrenched for many generations, a family has the option of overcoming these pointless, energy-wasting power struggles rather than just passing them on to the next generation. When a family recognizes the particular dynamics at work within their own family, and understands why the power struggles have resulted, they are able to discover who they really are, allowing the power struggles to fall away and the lives of all the family members to truly blossom.

The basis for the four personality classifications is a person not being in tune with the infinite energy of the universe, thus having to rely upon and manipulate the man-made energy that we discussed in chapter two. This is how an individual receives the energy, (or attention), from others within their family. A dominant classification is learned, primarily from parents, very early in our family life and spans a spectrum from aggressive to passive. The order of the spectrum is as follows:

1. The Intimidator: These individuals use the threat of verbal or bodily harm to gain their energy and control from family members. Intimidators usually create "Poor Me" family members, but also can create other intimidators who chose to fight back.

2. The Interrogator: These individuals control and gain their energy from their family members by finding fault and criticizing them after asking constant questions and prob-

ing into others' business. Interrogators create "Aloof" family members as they become distant while attempting to avoid the interrogation.

3. <u>The Aloof</u>: These individuals as parents were either absentee family members or ignored you due to preoccupation with other activities, career, etc. Aloof parents create "Interrogators" as children, who are forced into this to get answers out of the aloof parents.

4. <u>The Poor Me</u>: These individuals gain their energy and control others by gaining their sympathy. They commonly take a very passive approach and tell others how terrible things are for them. Poor Me individuals have the potential to create any of the other three classifications, as family members constantly defend themselves from the idea that they are not to blame for the Poor Me.

Currently in our society, families are faced with more difficulties than ever. As each family member becomes conscious of their family dynamic, they begin to understand why the power struggles exist and why certain family problems have developed. As they begin to see this picture more clearly, they can all move closer to becoming more dynamic and balanced individuals, and this in turn will give us more dynamic and balanced families.

5. Mental

The mental area of life is a never-ending pursuit, especially when it has been estimated that we only use 10% of our brain capacity. We certainly have a long way to go! Growth in this area includes continuing education, reading, self-help cassette tapes, imagination, recall, logic, attitude, curiosity, etc. Physical and mental subluxations may manifest in this area of life as loss of imagination, depression, paranoia, phobias, loss of ambition, pessimism, loss of reasoning and logic, overall decreased mental activity and many other manifestations.

This is where we start to shift our conscious awareness into a state of "abundance and prosperity," as we will discuss in chapter six. As it becomes ingrained in our subconscious awareness, truly powerful things begin to happen to our lives. It is up to us to constantly feed our minds daily with the positive. If not, our society will see to it that we will be filled with the negative. It seems unfair, but it takes no effort to be filled with the negative. However, it takes constant focus, determination and love on our part to become filled with the positive and remain there.

I recommend to individuals that they attempt to read at least two books per month and to never have a period when they are "between books" for any length of time. The day you finish one book is the day you start another. Additionally, due to our fast-paced society, where our cars are becoming our home away from home, we must take advantage of the learning possibilities through cassette tapes. I recommend to individuals to turn down the negative talk radio shows and turn up a self-help cassette tape. You will soon notice the positive results manifesting in your life. *You are what you are and where you are, because of what you have put into your mind!*

6. Career

The career area of life includes one's chosen vocation in life, whether it is a nine-to-five office job, a volunteer position, a child-rearing head of a household, or any other activity that one decides to spend their life doing. Growth in this area includes knowledge or expertise of your vocation, continued improvement and advancement, job satisfaction, salary, benefits, effectiveness, job training, competence, purpose, etc. Physical and mental subluxations in this area of life may manifest as a consistent failure to accomplish career objectives and goals, a non-challenging or personally non-engaging career environment, an inability to grasp the knowledge or expertise of the career, a lack of continued improvement and advancement, a lack of career satisfaction or fulfillment and many others.

It is my belief that we live in a universe where we can choose work that we love to do and by doing so, we are fully supported by the universe, creating unlimited abundance on whatever level we desire. But, when it comes to career and work, our society has perpetrated one of the biggest lies that humankind has ever been taught. Society daily exposes us to the mindset of going through the weekly grind of our jobs, so we can pay the bills to survive in our physical existence. Bills, I might add, that a materialistic and over-commercialized society has a *huge* financial stake in.

We are persuaded through a bombardment of advertising, that this is okay because we should only "live for the weekend." Or that we should put in our twenty years of service so we can qualify for the gold watch and finally reach the "ultimate goal" of retirement. It is then, we are told, that true happiness and true fulfillment will finally be ours, and we can sail off into the sunset. But this is not what happens. When we get to this sunset we find that our boat is leaking! We find out that we were living a tremendous lie, waiting for some unforeseen happiness down the road, when we should have been enjoying the ride all along.

We have lost the real purpose of what work was meant to be for us. Work was meant to be an expression to the world of who we really are. Interestingly enough, if you currently find you are in work that does not fit this criteria, then you are actually working in and taking another individual's job; an individual whose true expression to the world would be doing the job you currently are occupying. How is that for a guilt trip!

Furthermore, many individuals have told me how much they hate or dislike their work. They feel trapped by their work and justify staying because of financial reasons. They are clinging to a security that is mediocre at best. *Those who stay in a job they hate are doubly penalized. Not only do they despise their work, but worse yet, it doesn't even make them wealthy!*

Each of us has within us a unique and special talent that belongs only to us. This special talent or gift is given from the universe and is given to us because it is needed at this particular time on our planet. The universe never gives illusory gifts, or, in other words, gifts with no purpose, or are not needed by our planet. Universal law is such that when we have been given a special gift or talent, it is always accompanied by an unlimited abundance of others on our planet who need and want our special gift or talent. This also means that we will be abundantly supported, financial or otherwise, on any level that we desire in return for our gifts and talents. The bottom line to all this and a mindset I attempt to convey to individuals is this: *IF YOU ARE NOT USING YOUR SPECIAL GOD-GIVEN TALENT OR GIFT, YOU ARE BEING EXTREMELY SELFISH TO THE REST OF US, AND YOU ARE CHEATING THE ENTIRE PLANET OUT OF YOUR PURPOSE FOR EXISTENCE!*

When individuals move into a career that utilizes their unique gifts and talents, the universe begins to support and reward you in ways you would have never imagined. We move into alignment with the spirit of the universe and our career becomes one in which we love and which transforms our planet. This is what is called our Divine Purpose by many of our spiritual traditions, and our reward for following it is a life of unlimited abundance and prosperity.

7. Spiritual

The spiritual area of life should not be confused with the spiritual plane of existence! The spiritual area of life is one of the seven areas of the physical and mental planes of existence and involves our conscious physical connection to the spirit in our lives. Growth in this area should include religious/spiritual study, belief in God, church involvement, spiritual guidance for family, continued growth in faith, inner peace, prayer/meditation, sense of purpose, etc. Physical and mental subluxations in this area of life may manifest as a loss of purpose, an inner turmoil, persistent restlessness, a loss of "centeredness" or "grounding", chaos throughout the other six areas of life and many other conditions along this line.

A failure to strive for a conscious physical connection to the spiritual in our lives is seen all around us in today's society. This is the individual with the deep inner void that never gets filled. This void leads one on a perpetual chase away from the connection to spirit and into the awaiting arms of perceived "security" or "happiness" throughout our physical world. Whether this is the next new sports car, the better and bigger house, the next "new and improved" wife or husband, a greater amount of money in the bank or the latest miracle cosmetic surgical technique; these individuals find that the inner void just keeps getting bigger and bigger.

Ancient civilizations stressed their physical connection to the spiritual much more than we do in today's society. We see it in recent archaeological finds, as they have unearthed massive and monumental temples and palaces where spiritual practices were held. These temples and palaces were certainly the largest structures in their society and must have dwarfed the other buildings and dwellings within their municipalities, cities and villages.

I am ashamed about what tomorrow's archaeologists will dig up 500 years from now as they seek clues into what we valued as important as a culture. The largest and most massive "temples" and "palaces" of our day that will be unearthed will say Neiman Marcus, The Galleria, or The Mall of the Americas. I think at first the archaeologists will be puzzled, but then I think they will only feel sorry for us.

Consistent success in these seven areas can only be achieved with the absence of physical or mental subluxations, allowing the spirit within the body to become attuned with the spirit of the universe. Chiropractic should always evaluate an individual in all seven areas of life. Successful areas will be identified as well as any areas that are lacking. Many times I have found that it is a great revelation to the individual when they learn about the seven areas and they immediately begin striving for growth in all areas. This new found awareness can be the biggest step of all.

One more note on the seven areas of life within our physical and mental existence. The seven areas are what many of our current spiritual writers and thinkers are terming "an illusion." They stress that the physical does not really exist as we have thought and that it should never deserve our focus. I am in total agreement with them. We are spiritual beings, temporarily experiencing the physical and mental existence, and it is pointless to focus our lives on a physical existence that is only temporary.

However, many of these current spiritual writers and thinkers fail to recognize the absolute usefulness and the extraordinary blessing our physical existence has on our spiritual lives. Unfortunately, I think it is possible for individuals to become so "spiritual" that they become no "earthly good," and this is something to be avoided. Sure, the physical existence is a temporary illusion, but at our current state of consciousness and evolution, the apparent success or failure in each of our seven areas of life provides one of the few "barometers" of an individual's spiritual health within. Illusion or not, we are absolutely meant to enjoy all the rich blessings of our physical world. This can only be accomplished with the absence of subluxations, providing a maximum expression of spirit within as it travels above, down, inside and out.

We will now discuss why it is absolutely crucial that we consistently achieve growth in all seven areas of our lives. We will learn how we can consciously create this growth and what chiropractic can do to help. And lastly we will see that much of this process in the next chapter will require a great deal of the burden to be shifted off the chiropractor and placed solely on the individual if this growth is to be achieved.

Notes

Chapter Six
<u>If We Are Not Growing,</u>
<u>We Are Dying</u>

"Where there is no vision, the people perish; but he that keepeth the law, happy is he."
Proverbs 29:18

"Either get busy living or get busy dying."
Andy DuFresne in the movie
The Shawshank Redemption

"If a person advances confidently in the direction of one's dreams and endeavors to live the life they have imagined, they will meet with success unexpected in common hours."
Henry David Thoreau

According to universal law, when an object within our universe is not growing, thriving and expanding, it is slowly but surely dying. Unfortunately, there is no "in-between" here and a blissful life of eternal mediocrity is not an option for us. Realizing this, we see that our purpose here on earth is so much bigger than just paying the bills, living for the weekend, getting the kids through college, accumulating 401K accounts and wishing for retirement. When these ideals become our focus, we are no longer growing and expanding; rather, we are slowly but surely dying inside.

The reason for this is because we exist in a growing, thriving and expanding universe. The Inflationary Theory of the universe states that new stars, planets, solar systems and galaxies are continually being created every day. It says that the natural state of our universe is a state of dynamic flux, never remaining static, and that there is no end to the continued expansion of the universe.

We as human beings are no different and must continually strive for growth and expansion if we are to remain in alignment with the universe. It is my belief that many of our problems arise when the expansion of the individual does not keep pace with the expansion of the universe! I feel Jesus was explaining this "growth or death" concept, as well as the universe's patience with us, with his parable of the fig tree:

> *"There once was a person who had a fig tree planted in his orchard, and when he came in search for fruit on it but found none, he said to the gardener, "For three years now I have come in search of fruit on this fig tree but have found none. So cut it down. Why should it exhaust the soil?" He said to him in reply, "Sir leave it for this year also, and I shall cultivate the ground around it and fertilize it; it may bear fruit in the future. If not you can cut it down."*
> *(Luke 13:6)*

This "grow or die" philosophy has always been embraced

by chiropractic and is conveyed to all patients. The location in which this growth is achieved by us is within the seven areas of life which were discussed in the last chapter. Although the chiropractor is always available to teach and assist individuals with this growth process, this is ultimately where much of the burden is shifted off the chiropractor and on to the individual. Much is required of the individual during this process, with true consistent growth and expansion only occurring through conscious, self-aware, hard work on the part of the individual. This is one of the times mentioned in this book where it is ultimately dependent solely on the individual to align *themselves* with the universe.

Growth is scary stuff. I compare it to walking a tightrope in the circus without a net below to catch us. It requires us to stretch ourselves as human beings, abandon our comfort zones, and reach heights that were previously thought impossible. Then we find, upon reaching these new heights, we are amazed that they were ever thought unreachable to us. Thereupon, we immediately set our sights on even greater heights with a new-found, ever-increasing level of confidence.

This is true growth, and it is the natural state that human beings were sent to earth to experience. This state places us in perfect alignment with our growing, expanding universe, and we are filled with an unmistakably fulfilling feeling within us as our growing aligns us with the universe. We truly receive a feeling of being totally "alive" within our lives.

Upon experiencing this feeling, many people remark that it is something that they have never experienced before. However, this is simply not true. This is the natural feeling that we all had throughout our childhood, even though we may have "grown up" and forgotten. This feeling is the result of connecting with the inexhaustible and infinite energy of the universe discussed in chapter two. Instinctively, children, who are fresh from the spiritual plane, know of no better energy source to connect to. It is we adults who forget.

Growth Through Goal Setting

The only way we can achieve any type of consistent growth within our lives, is when we have charted a course and identified an ultimate destination for our lives. With an ultimate destination, the inevitable short term failures that present in our lives prove to be a pebble on the seashore instead of an insurmountable mountain in our way. This is the process of goal setting, and chiropractic has always taught this vital tool for our lives.

Goal setting, when performed properly, enables dreams to come true in individual's lives. A famous study was performed at Yale University in 1953 on the graduating seniors. The study discovered that just 3% of the class properly performed goal-setting procedures. Conversely, they found 97% of the class either did not set any type of goals or took insufficient steps in the goal-setting process.

Twenty years later, in 1973, they interviewed the same class again. In terms of the two areas of life which are easiest to measure, career and financial, they found an astonishing result. *The previous 3% of the class who properly set goals had accomplished more than the remaining 97% combined!*

As our vehicle for growth, goal setting is not a "hit and miss" endeavor. When performed properly, utilizing all the steps, goal setting is an absolute science, having the power to manifest anything you desire. Goal setting is how we communicate with our universe by conceiving of what, where, and how we want to live. As we spoke about in chapter two, all of our thoughts, emotions, and feelings interact with the vibration of our universe. It is up to us to make the impact of our vibration positive or negative. *GOAL SETTING IS SIMPLY THE POSITIVE VIBRATORY PROJECTION OF OUR DESIRES INTO THE UNIVERSE AND THE FAITH THAT THE UNIVERSE WILL HANDLE THE DETAILS AND BRING THEM FORTH!*

Although much of the work of goal setting is left up to the individual, the chiropractor is available to stress the importance of this vital growth process and assist in defining clear-cut and concise goals. These goals are both short term and long term, and they "chart the course" for the individual's life direction.

The chiropractor's assistance in goal setting is many times a much needed catalyst in today's hectic, fast-paced society. Unfortunately, it is incredible but true that most people spend more time planning a vacation than they do planning their lives. Furthermore, many of us treat the Macy's catalog far better than our lives. When we place a catalog order we specifically state every detail about the item we desire. But when it comes to the rest of our lives, many of us seem content to just say to the universe, *Just give me something you think I might like!* No wonder so many individuals go through life disappointed.

The Twelve Steps to Goals of Abundance and Prosperity

Just writing our desires down on paper, however, is not enough to reach our goals, (even though this is still better than a majority of society). There are proper steps that are necessary for goal setting to be successful, and the chiropractor is available to educate the individual on these vital steps. When clear goals are listed and all the steps are followed, our goals are quickly attained.

The following is a brief rundown of the twelve steps to goals of abundance and prosperity. These steps are necessary for successful goal setting and attainment. A brief summary is included under most of the steps.

1. Prepare a dream sheet. This is the fun part! Take some time to be alone in a quiet place and just start listing everything you plan to have, be, do, share and create. This list should contain a healthy balance of desires throughout each of the seven areas of life and they should be listed right down to the smallest detail. Just go crazy and write everything, no matter how seemingly far-fetched or inconceivable. Start writing and do not stop until you cannot possibly think of another desire.

IT IS EXTREMELY IMPORTANT TO THINK BIG. Remember the old story about the man who died and met St. Peter in heaven. They looked around at what St. Peter called the heavenly junk yard, as St. Peter explained, "Here you'll find all the gifts from heaven that people on earth rejected."

"Why that's impossible!" the man replied, "Some of these gifts are beautiful. Look at that Cadillac over there. Who could have rejected that?"

"Well, it is interesting you ask about that car," replied St. Peter. "The person who rejected that Cadillac is you."

"Impossible! I'd never have refused such a wonderful gift," the man exclaimed.

"Yes, it was you. You see, the Cadillac was ready to be delivered to you. But every time you prayed for a car, you kept visualizing a little Volkswagen!"

This is wonderful advice for us to always remember to think big. Daniel H. Burnham says it best, *Make no small plans; they do nothing to stir man's blood.*

2. Reassess your dream sheet. For each of the items listed you should be able to clearly articulate why you would want it and how it would benefit you. Each item listed also must be totally under your control and not dependent upon other people having to change themselves for you. In addition, each item listed must benefit you and other people without harming any person, place or thing. If all these criteria fit your listed items, they are truly goals ready for attainment with the full support of the universe behind you.

3. Put a date on them. Decide on what date you would be willing to receive each of these goals: six months, one year, two years, five years, ten years, etc. This is also helpful to see what type of time frame your consciousness is operating in (short term, long term, etc.).

4. Choose the seven most significant goals for you to accomplish this year.

5. Look within. Ask what must you change about yourself in order to receive these goals by this date. Listen and watch for your answer.

6. Take positive action in faith. This step includes an identification of three different elements. 1) Identify potential obstacles. 2) Identify potential helpful resources (people, groups, organizations, etc.). 3) Identify the knowledge and skills you will need.

Keep in mind that, with this particular step, *the universe always handles the details after we have become clear on our desires.* Although we are identifying our own personal plan of action, goals are very often attained by circumstances we had no way of predicting. In my opinion, we are rewarded for beginning our personal action steps even though they may or may not be needed.

Remember Joshua and the Israelites as they crossed the Jordan River. The waters did not part until they stepped into the water and got their feet wet (Joshua 3:15). In other words, it took a positive action in faith on their part before they were rewarded.

7. Accept and imagine your success now. In other words, *act as if.* For example, with travel goals, get new luggage if necessary, see yourself boarding the airplane, or picture yourself at the Eiffel Tower.

8. Read goals frequently. Read your goals at least three time a day. This creates focus and concentration upon your goals. Always make one of the three readings the last thing you do before going to sleep. This triggers the subconscious dream state to go to work on your goals. When you begin this practice, always keep a pen and paper beside your bed to record your dreams whenever possible. You will be greatly assisted by the wealth of ideas that bubble up from the subconscious every night.

9. Don't tell others. The one exception would be loving, trusting, supportive individuals who can think and believe as big as you can.

10. Have an attitude of gratitude. Become the most thankful, confident, and enthusiastic person you know. Always remember, the universe does not give further blessings to individuals who are ungrateful for what they have.

11. Edit regularly. Cross off goals as they are achieved and continue to add new ones. It is perfectly natural to change your mind on goals from time to time. If a goal ceases to be a desire for you and no longer motivates you, cross it off and replace it with a new desire that does. Always remember that our desires are not of our own choosing. The word *de-sire* means *of the Father,* or *from the Father.* When a desire is implanted within our consciousness by the Father, who are we to question it?

12. 10% goes to the universe. Throughout the Old Testament and other sacred texts, the number ten was considered by ancient civilizations to be a mystical symbol of increase. In order for an individual to achieve abundance and prosperity, or to maintain their current level of success, they gave one-tenth of their income to God. In the words of Solomon, *"I will honor the Lord with my substance and with the first fruits of all my increase"* (Proverbs 3:9).

However, it is not stated anywhere that this 10% gift has to go to a church, religious organization, preacher, or any other religiously affiliated recipient. This very powerful and ancient law has been the victim of much misuse, deception and greed in recent years. Because of this, many people have turned away from this powerful law and the tremendous good which it can create.

In actuality, this 10% gift was meant for the person, places and organizations that serve as our spiritual teachers and further our spiritual growth. We are rewarding the recipients of our gifts for opening our eyes to truth, no matter who they are. Just as easily as a religious institution, these recipients may also be an elderly gentleman in the park, a waitress in a diner, a spiritual study group, an author of a book, or even a chiropractor. This is my view of our world culture in the next millennium. As we evolve into a spiritual economy, our incomes will derive from evolving freely and offering our unique truth to others.

One more note about this 10% gift for the universe. The funniest thing about this law is that we all follow it no matter what. If we refuse to honor this ancient law, the universe simply takes its share anyway through car repairs, unexpected bills, sudden family expenses, and many others. When you try to "save money" and withhold your gifts, it seems to "cost" you more than the original 10% gift would have been!

The Pain of Regret

We have just read about our absolute need to consistently grow as human beings in order to remain in alignment with the consistent growth of our universe. We have also read that our growth must take place within all seven areas of life equally, and the only way this is successfully accomplished is through goal setting. It is a certainty that if we follow the proper steps of goal setting, we can manifest our desires. However, it is now necessary to briefly discuss the consequences of failing or refusing to consistently grow as human beings.

As we discussed earlier, the alternative to growth is a slow, gradual death. But along with death comes another terribly painful state; a state that destroys individuals from the inside-out and makes them wish for another chance. This would be the pain of regret.

This is what is meant when it is said that *most human beings go to their graves with their music still in them.* The pain of regret results from a refusal to grow as a human being and a wasting of the universe's gifts. When it comes to growth, remember, *the pain of discipline is minuscule compared to the pain of regret.*

The pain of regret presents itself, sometimes on one's deathbed, after a realization occurs of just how incredible our gifts from the universe really were. It is a miserable feeling of *what if,* that permeates our existence regarding the missed opportunities throughout all seven areas of our life. It is finally seen exactly what was given to us and it was up to us all along to develop these gifts into something greater.

I feel our decision to grow, or our decision to "play it safe" and essentially waste the resources given to us, is exactly what Jesus meant in his parable of the talents:

"It will be as when a man who was going on a journey called in his servants and entrusted his possessions to them. To one he gave five talents; to another, two; to a third, one-to each according to his ability. Then he went away. Immediately the one who received five talents went and traded with them, and made another five. Likewise, the one who received two made another two. But the man who received one went off and dug a hole in the ground and buried his master's money.

After a long time the master of those servants came back and settled accounts with them. The one who had received five talents came forward bringing the additional five. He said, 'Master, you gave me five talents. See, I have made five more.' His master said to him, 'Well done, my good and faithful servant. Since you were faithful in small matters, I will give you great responsibilities. Come, share your master's joy.'

Then the one who had received two talents also came forward and said, 'Master, you gave me two talents. See, I have made two more.' His master said to him, 'Well done my good and faithful servant. Since you were faithful in small matters, I will give you great responsibilities. Come, share your master's joy.'

Then the one who had received one talent came forward and said, 'Master, I knew you were a demanding person, harvesting where you did not plant and gathering where you did not scatter; so out of fear I went off and buried your talent in the ground. Here it is back.' His master said to him in reply, 'You wicked, lazy servant! So you knew that I harvest where I did not plant and gather where I did not scatter? Should you not then have put my money in the bank so that I could have got it back with interest on my return? Now then! Take the talent from him and give it to the one with ten. For to everyone who has, more will be given and he will grow rich; but from the one who has not, even what he has will be taken away. And throw this useless servant into the darkness outside, where there will be wailing and grinding of teeth" (Matthew 25:14).

Our decision to consciously grow and expand as human beings and align with our growing and expanding universe will be supported in ways that cannot be imagined. This growth and expansion can only be achieved by setting clear, concise goals and following the twelve steps for their attainment. A growing and expanding state is who we truly are as human beings, and chiropractic is there to help.

Although the process of growth is scary and requires some pain of discipline, it pales in comparison to the pain of regret. Now let us discuss what is possible for us when our growth and expansion has aligned us with the abundant spirit of the universe. Now let us discuss the powerful abundance and prosperity that awaits us when we have a maximally expressed spirit within our nervous system combined with a conscious awareness of growth and expansion.

Notes

Chapter Seven
Alignment To Spirit Within — Lives of Abundance and Prosperity

"Fear not little flock, for it is the Father's good pleasure to give you the kingdom."
Luke 12:32

Throughout this book you will hear the terms "abundance and prosperity" used quite often. I use the terms abundance and prosperity to describe the perfect and ultimate state of consciousness and being to which we are all striving as human beings. The state of abundance and prosperity occurs when we have a maximum expression of the spirit of the universe flowing through us, above, down, inside and out. The result of living in a state of abundance and prosperity is when all seven areas of our life in the physical and mental plane flow perfectly, as we seem to "effortlessly" go through our physical world guided by our spirit within.

The term abundance is simply the natural state of affairs in our universe. The term prosperity is the result we experience when we adopt abundance consciousness. Prosperity can manifest in any of the seven areas of life and can encompass such things as a healthy body that we are maximally expressing our spirit through, relationships that are joyous, intimate, honest and supportive, work that we love that is transforming our planet, financial abundance, and numerous other manifestations within the seven areas of life.

Although it is possible to have forgotten, the true nature of our being is one of unlimited abundance and prosperity. We currently live in the midst of an incredibly lavish and abundant universe that allows us to be, do, or have absolutely anything we desire. In fact, to the degree that we are not experiencing total abundance in each and every area of our life, is the degree to which we are pushing it away or holding it back! This is certainly hard to fathom for individuals who currently are experiencing life's difficulties. In fact, none of us are immune to the occasional forgetting of the lavishness and abundance of our universe when we experience a difficulty in our physical existence. But this is when we must remember exactly who we really are.

We are spiritual beings created in the image and likeness of the Most High. If we believe this scriptural promise, then we come to a stark realization. This is the realization that we do not glorify God when we are sick, when we live in poverty, when we do not perform loving work that transforms the planet, when we carry around feelings of guilt, when we go through life as a "victim," or when we simply fail to become a "light" in our corner of the world for others to see. In fact, these could be considered selfish acts on our part when we fall into their grip.

The consciousness of living in an abundant universe is a crucial truth that chiropractic has always stressed. It is fascinating to see that many on our planet do not have this consciousness, but a belief system of limitation and lack, which is underlying much of society's ills, (crime, war, poverty, illness, etc.). This is because when the belief system is limitation and lack, it will not be long before the outer world shows you exactly that. My favorite phrase in this regard is, *Your innermost dominant thought becomes your outermost tangible reality.*

I included as one of society's ills the one aspect that many spiritual individuals have a difficult time embracing and personally claiming for themselves. This is the aspect of financial abundance. As spiritual individuals, when we avoid wealth, we are being *extremely selfish*! We are selfish in the fact that we are giving away the power to decide how the resources of the planet are to be used. We are giving this power to others who are spending the wealth in ways that are contrary to our spiritual ideals. Chiropractic recognizes that it is our temporary physical and mental existences that have the potential to block this incredible good. We must make the decision not to be selfish and to maximize the amount of abundance and prosperity we manifest in our lives.

I read an article a while back regarding abundance consciousness, in which they interviewed ten millionaires about their beliefs. Every single one of them had in common the belief that there is an unlimited supply of money to be made in this world, and that it is always available if we want it. I also read that someone asked Henry Ford, the titan of the automotive industry, what would happen if tomorrow he would lose his entire fortune. To the amazement of the interviewer, Ford calmly and confidently replied that he would simply find another need in our society and fill that need more efficiently and with greater quality than anyone else. He was absolutely confident his fortune would certainly be regained in a short while. And we have all heard it conjectured that if all the money in the world were divided up equally among the inhabitants of the planet, in just five short years the money would be returned to the original affluent people that had the money in the first place! This is the abundance and prosperity consciousness.

It is a known fact that if you have food to eat at all three meals, a car to drive, clothes to wear, and a home to live in, you are in the top 95% of the world's overall wealth! This is certainly something for which we should all be very thankful, but it is also reason to be very disheartened. This tells me that 95% of our planet does not believe that we live in an abundant universe. Please do not take this to mean that we should not show compassion for others less fortunate on our planet, because we certainly should. What I am saying is that there is a better way; a way that empowers us to see for ourselves that the true essence of our universe is one of unlimited abundance and prosperity.

We will never have to worry about abundance and prosperity in our spiritual planes of existence. As truly spiritual beings, we are already the most remarkable, splendid creation in God's universe. It has always been that way and it will always be that way. What we have to watch out for is the physical and mental planes of our existence, which have the potential to get in the way of our true spiritual essence. The role of chiropractic is to empower the individual to manifest abundance and prosperity in their lives, by removing all interference from the physical and mental planes of existence.

This is accomplished by the removal of the subluxations that are blocking the expression of the spirit of the universe within us. These subluxations "sabotage" the seven areas of our lives and limit the degree to which we experience abundance and prosperity. When these subluxations are removed, we move toward a more maximal expression of the spirit within as it runs through us above, down, inside and out.

We will next discuss the other choice we have when it comes to the spirit of the universe within our nervous systems. This is the choice of just how we as human beings can block or "subluxate" the spirit within and affect the seven areas of life within our physical and mental existence.

Notes

Chapter Eight
Getting in the Way of Spirit Within — The Subluxated Nervous System

"Full, rich, and abounding health is the normal and the natural condition of life. Anything else is an abnormal condition, and abnormal conditions as a rule come through perversions. God never created sickness, suffering, and disease; they are man's own creations. They come through his violating the laws under which he lives.

...No man's success or health will ever reach beyond his own confidence; as a rule, we erect our own barriers."
    Ralph Waldo Trine from In Tune With The Infinite, 1899.

   The true spiritual aspect of ourselves and our connection to the spirit of the universe as it is expressed in us from above, down, inside and out, is what this entire book is about. We have already seen that living our lives as the spiritual beings we are, and allowing that spirit to guide our lives, creates an existence of abundance and prosperity in our lives. This is who we were when we existed in the spiritual plane, and it is the natural state of who we are now during our existence in the physical and mental planes as well.

However, when we experience and see illness, poverty, chaos, and other difficulties in life, the most obvious question is this: "If we are these perfect spiritual beings, why don't our lives just work perfectly all the time?" After asking this question myself on occasion, I have come to a big realization:

OUR LIVES ARE EXACTLY THE WAY THEY ARE BECAUSE OF THE CHOICES WE HAVE MADE, CONSCIOUSLY OR SUBCONSCIOUSLY!

Although we are truly spiritual beings, it is the temporary physical and mental planes of our existence that contain the potential to create blockages to the spirit of the universe within our nervous systems. In chiropractic, these blockages are called "subluxations," and the primary role of chiropractic is the detection and removal of these subluxations.

These subluxations can either be physical subluxations or mental subluxations, with both being detrimental to the flow of the spirit of the universe within us. When this occurs, we become "un-attuned" with the universe around us, and we lessen our connection to our true spiritual selves. This prevents a maximal connection to our spiritual selves, leading to a failure to live up to our truest potential. This is where we see creations such as dis-ease, chaos, illness, poverty, and many other undesirable conditions within the seven areas of life.

As we spoke about earlier, this is absolutely a choice each individual has to make. The choice of experiencing lives of abundance and prosperity on the physical and mental planes, or the choice of suffering and struggling through existence, by failing to wake up and recognize their true spiritual nature. The purpose of chiropractic is to assist in making the right decision, by evaluating and removing subluxations from the physical and mental planes of existence, and providing a maximum expression of the spirit of the universe within an individual's nervous system.

Now, when I talk of the spirit being blocked by physical and mental subluxations, I am never implying that spirit is totally being blocked from running our bodies. That would be impossible because spirit is what we are. The block of spirit caused by subluxations is merely a "less than maximal" expression of spirit. One individual with a major subluxation may be expressing 65% of the maximal expression of the spirit of life, whereas an individual with a minor subluxation may be expressing 80% of his human spiritual potential. It all boils down to how much of your potential do you want to express in your life. Once again, it is our choice, and no choice is right or wrong.

I remember as a college student I was torn between going to medical school or going to chiropractic school. The primary factor in my decision to become a chiropractor was chiropractic's philosophy of ADIO, and a question that I could not get answered by the medical community. The question that I posed to them was this. Consider the idea of two comparably healthy and physically identical individuals sitting next to each other in the same room. At this time they are both exposed to the same flu bug. Why does one get sick and the other one remain just fine?

Now, according to the medical model of health, this flu bug is considered our enemy and must be eradicated at all costs through medications, vaccines, and other medical procedures. So, if the medical "enemy flu bug" concept were correct, shouldn't this flu bug be equally dangerous to both individuals in that room? Something is missing here!

The thing that is missing is "a mysterious something" that is within the well individual, allowing the flu bug to have no affect on him. Chiropractic recognizes this "mysterious something." Chiropractic's philosophy of ADIO explains that the well individual was "stronger" inside by having a larger expression of his spirit flowing through him, than the sick person who was physically or mentally subluxating the expression of his spirit flowing in him. It is very possible that the well individual was expressing 75% of his spirit and the sick individual was expressing 65%. The difference between wellness and disease may only be a mere 10%.

What it all comes down to is a simple choice. The hard learned lessons from lives of dis-ease, chaos, struggle and poverty are not at all necessary and are strictly optional. We are certainly free to have these hard learned lessons if we truly want them. But chiropractic exists to show us that there is a better choice to make and shows us how to do it. Chiropractic helps us to choose lives of abundance and prosperity that result from having a maximum expression of the spirit of the universe flowing through our nervous systems.

We shall now talk about the physical subluxation and how it is one of the ways we can block or subluxate our spirit.

Chapter Nine
The Physical Subluxation

"In the first place, the structure of the spine should be known, for this knowledge is requisite in many diseases."
                              Hippocrates, The Father of Medicine, 400 B.C.

You only have to look at the human body to see where the universe's priorities lie. Nature in her infinite wisdom knew which part of the body was the most crucial to our function. Not only is the nervous system the first to develop in a fetus, but after development this system is almost entirely encased in bone unlike any other organ or system of our body. That is because it is the housing for the spirit of the universe within us, and it is to be protected at all costs.

The only other organ of the body that remotely has the same complexity of structural protection is the heart. Surrounded by the sternum and rib cage, it is evident the universe wanted the heart protected at all costs also. The universe's design of protecting the heart was to safeguard the very area where our love is expressed, enabling us to align with the infinite universal energy that we discussed in chapter two. The protection of the nervous system safeguards the very area that the spirit in life is expressed as we experience our physical and mental world. It could be argued that expressing our love and expressing our spirit in life are the two primary purposes and reasons for being on the planet.

Unfortunately, it is also this protective bone covering of the nervous system that occasionally is subjected to minor impingements or blockages from time to time due to structural misalignments of these bones. This is an example of a physical subluxation. It partially alters or blocks the maximum expression of spirit within the spinal cord. This physical subluxation can best be illustrated by our garden hose example. Imagine the hose being turned all the way on, but as the flow of water gushes toward a "kink" in the hose, it results in a tiny trickle of water coming out of the end of the hose. This trickle of water is what happens to the spirit within the spinal cord after trying to pass through the "kink" or the physical subluxation (see figure 9.1).

As the spirit within the spinal cord is lessened by a physical subluxation, an individual becomes overcome and susceptible to an external environment that normally should be co-existing in a homeostatic relationship with the human body. The result of this physical subluxation is any one or more of a variety of problems within the seven areas of life that gradually manifest in the individual. It is a direct result of becoming "un-attuned" with the universe around us.

As an individual suffers in all seven areas of the physical experience of their existence, conditions such as dis-ease, chaos, fatigue, relationship difficulties, poverty, depression, ac-

THE PHYSICAL SUBLUXATION

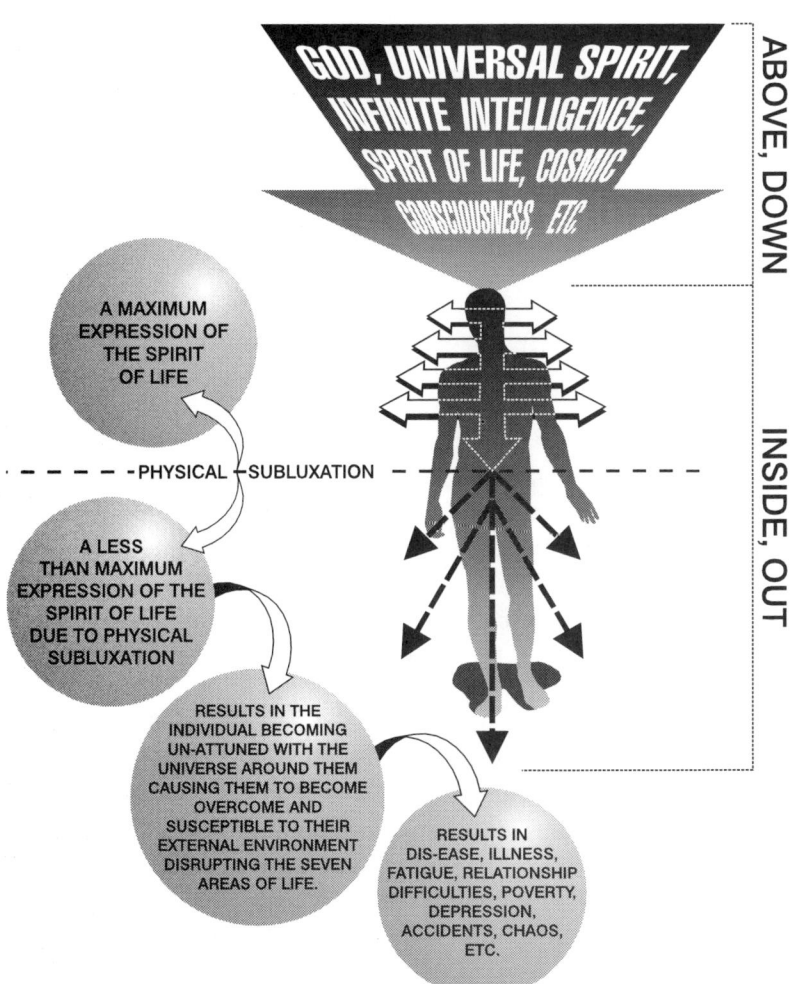

FIGURE 9.1

cidents, etc., manifest themselves. The human body's homeostatic relationship with our universe is lost and disharmony is always the end result.

Correction of the Physical Subluxation

The practice of chiropractic has always centered on the evaluation of the spine for subluxations. In addition, after fully evaluating the spine, a chiropractor will then evaluate the other physical joints of the body and determine if a physical subluxation exists. After evaluation, a physical subluxation is corrected through a gentle manipulation, or adjustment, of the joint to restore it back into its normal position.

An adjustment is painless and takes just a few minutes to accomplish. Depending on the individual's history of physical deterioration, overall health, and their faith in the treatment, one or more adjustments may be necessary to stabilize the joint and allow it to remain in its normal position. Physical subluxations are formed gradually over a period of time, and the correction comes gradually over a period of time.

It is interesting to mention at this time about a fascinating response our body has to chiropractic adjustments upon the correction of physical subluxations. The body has a deeply ingrained, subconscious memory pattern within, encompassing an entire lifetime, beginning with birth and possibly even with utero. As an individual receives corrective adjustments upon the physical subluxations, the body begins to "re-trace" many memory patterns of what has been experienced throughout their lifetime. For example, the physical body may dream of old injuries, symptoms or ailments as it "unlearns" the long standing and self-limiting subluxation patterns. *This may cause an individual to briefly experience symptoms that went away many years ago!* Although usually short lived, this response occurs as long as the body needs to hold the individual in a particular memory pattern, as it is learning to grow beyond the old physical subluxation patterns.

An adjustment is normally performed with a hands-on technique, but there are also many light-force techniques, including one where an adjusting instrument called an activator is used. All chiropractic techniques achieve the same purpose when removing physical subluxations; to free the flow of the spirit of the universe within an individual's previously physically subluxated nervous system. When accomplished, an individual moves closer to a maximum expression of the spirit of life, allowing greater human potential to manifest in all seven areas of life and moving ever closer to the ultimate state of spiritual lives of abundance and prosperity.

Law of Moderation

In addition to structural misalignment, a physical subluxation can occur another way. A physical subluxation blocking the spirit within the nervous system can occur when an individual violates an ancient law of wisdom. This law has been referred to down throughout the centuries by practically every great thinker who warned us against a violation. This is the ancient law of moderation.

The law of moderation simply states that anything done out of moderation, (eating, drinking, sleeping, working, etc., I could fill the pages of this book), will soon take their toll on an individual. Ultimately, it will adversely affect an individual's ability to achieve their true potential and maximize the expression of spirit within their lives.

The law of moderation is an extremely basic and simple law, not unlike all other great universal truths which are always basic and simple. It is almost as if the universe makes the most vital laws so simple that we cannot miss them. But, unfortunately, we do miss them, or simply disregard or ignore them. Many of our present societal and world woes of today could be improved or avoided altogether by simply obeying this law.

For the most part, the law of moderation sees the majority of our universe as neither good nor bad. The non-judgmental law of moderation says simply that our universe just "is". It is us as individuals who overutilize or underutilize the precious gifts of our universe and create the good and bad labels. Just as structural misalignments affect us, this overutilization or underutilization of our universe also creates physical subluxations that disrupt the human body's homeostatic relationship with our universe. As a result this manifests into disharmony within our lives as each of the seven areas of life is disrupted.

A chiropractor evaluates an individual's lifestyle for any violations of the law of moderation. Many times an individual has no conscious knowledge of overutilizing or underutilizing the gifts of the universe and violating the law of moderation. The chiropractor assists in this regard and many times facilitates a very enlightening experience for an individual. Chiropractic helps with the lifestyle changes that bring one back into moderation with the universe around them and eliminate the physical subluxation. This moves the individual closer to maximum expression of life by unleashing the spirit of the universe within them.

Now let us progress to one of the most damaging obstacles to a maximum expression to our spirit within; the mental subluxation.

Chapter Ten
The Mental Subluxation

"Man is the artificer of his own happiness."
                                        Henry David Thoreau

"Two men looked out from prison bars. One saw the mud, the other saw the stars!"
                                        Famous Proverb

   Most people are not in charge of their own thoughts and constantly bombard their true spiritual natures with a confusing and contradictory mixture of hopes, wishes, dreams and fears. This dangerous thought process, sometimes called mental subluxations, confuses the spiritual nature and results in people's lives being equally confusing and chaotic. Mental subluxations are the other way we as individuals can alter or block the spirit within our nervous systems and prevent lives of maximally expressed spirit.

When mental subluxations exist, we again become "unattuned" with the universe around us. As this occurs, just as with the physical subluxation, we become susceptible and overcome by our external environment, creating suffering in all seven areas of the physical experience. Again, conditions such as dis-ease, chaos, fatigue, relationship difficulties, poverty, depression, accidents and many others may manifest themselves.

Jesus said: *"Whoever loves his life will lose it. Whoever hates his life in this world will preserve it for eternity"* (John 12:25). This says it all for the power of our mental state and the effect upon our spirit within. Whoever loves his life, or, in other words, whoever has a positive outlook on life, shall lose his life and go on to greater rewards. But whoever hates his life, has a negative outlook, has excuses and consistently blames others, shall be condemned to this miserable state forever. In my opinion this would be a hell of their own creation.

A great story involves the parents of an optimist and a pessimist. At Christmas time the parents attempted to cure each one by giving the pessimist a room full of toys and the optimist a room full of manure. On Christmas morning they went into the pessimist's room and found him sitting in a corner. "What's the matter?" the parents asked. " I'm afraid to play with these toys. I might fall or get cut. It's safer to sit and watch," he replied. The frustrated parents then went into the optimist's room and found her throwing manure into the air, making little manure pies and basically having the time of her life. " What are you doing?" they asked. She happily responded, "With all this manure , there must be a pony in here somewhere!"

Our minds and our mental states determine to a large extent how much of the spirit of the universe we allow ourselves to receive. Staying true to the philosophy of ADIO, keep in mind that if our mental state is non receptive to spirit and essentially blocks spirit at the "Above, Down" phase, treatment of the spine would be fruitless. Spirit is being blocked before it reaches the spine, or, in other words, the "Inside, Out" phase (see figure 10.1). This is why the mental subluxation is more damaging than the physical subluxation.

Similar to the correction of the physical subluxation, the correction of the mental subluxation must also include the patient's faith and active participation in the process. When this occurs the correction is very powerful and when the mental subluxation is cleared, the possibilities of human potential are endless. The process of clearing the mental subluxation involves a choice. The choice to attune to the spirit or the choice to attune to the external environment. Jesus again says it best when he said, *"My kingdom does not belong to this world"* (John 18:36); and certainly this was what Paul was saying when he said, *"Do not conform yourself to this age but be transformed by the renewal of your mind"* (Romans 12:2).

Author, Bruce McArthur, in his book entitled, Your Life, explains in great detail the importance of attuning to spirit instead of the external environment. His work provided the inspiration for figure 10.2: A wonderful visualization to hold in mind when the temptation arises to focus on the external environment, or the world. A focus on our world will soon create mental subluxations, and chiropractic is there to help us return our focus back to spirit.

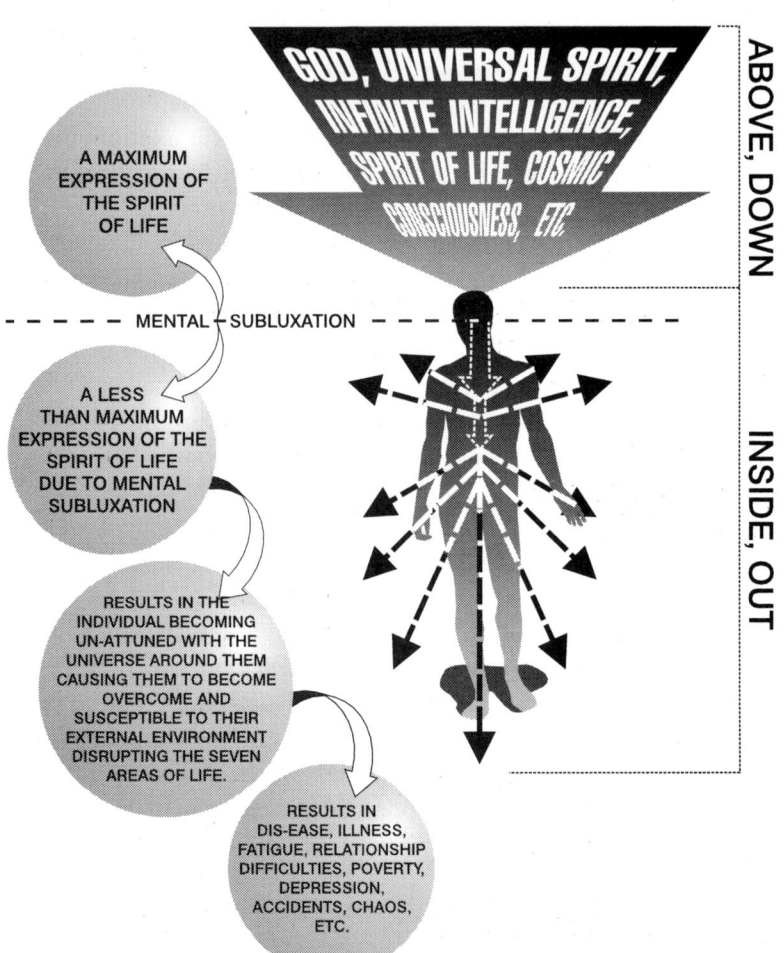

FIGURE 10.1

"Set your mind on heaven, and the earth will be thrown in.
Set your mind on the world, and you will receive neither."
C. S. Lewis

FIGURE 10.2

Correction of the Mental Subluxation

The mental subluxation is extremely more damaging to an individual than the physical subluxation and holds the potential to absolutely destroy an individual's seven areas of life. The mental subluxation blocks us from becoming beings of unlimited abundance and prosperity, which is who we truly are. The practice of chiropractic has always seen the importance of a patient's mental plane of existence. The evaluation of an individual always should include a check of any mental subluxations that are altering or blocking the spirit of the universe within that individual and preventing a maximum expression of their spiritual essence.

The primary task when evaluating the mental subluxation is determining an individual's most enduring and dominant thoughts and emotions, and then bringing them to the conscious awareness of the individual (see figures 10.3 and 10.4). Although it may require a deep self-honesty and self-discipline, an individual identifies and recognizes the predominant thought and emotional patterns. After this occurs the correction of the mental subluxation takes place by strengthening the positive patterns and replacing the negatives with positives, within a loving and supportive environment.

The chiropractor teaches the individual how to modify their lifestyle and to become aware of their emotions and thoughts. An individual is taught the absolute necessity of liking and loving themselves and the power of forgiveness and unconditional love. This allows the spirit of the universe to more fully express itself within us from above, down, inside and out. When we have a maximum expression of this spirit within our lives, we move into our rightful state of unlimited abundance and prosperity.

DOMINANT INNER "SELF TALK"

ABUNDANCE AND PROSPERITY CONSCIOUSNESS	MENTAL SUBLUXATION
EVERYDAY IN EVERY WAY I AM GETTING BETTER AND BETTER. I'M THE BEST.	I'M NOT GOOD ENOUGH
I FORGIVE MYSELF	I DESERVE PUNISHMENT
I LOVE MYSELF	I HATE MYSELF
I'M VERY DESERVING	I DON'T DESERVE
I AM NON-JUDGMENTAL	I JUDGE, CRITICIZE AND CONDEMN
I FORGIVE ALL OTHERS AND ALL CIRCUMSTANCES	I'LL NEVER FORGIVE HIM, HER OR THEM OR THAT UNFAIR CIRCUMSTANCE
I AM GOOD, SO I ATTRACT ALL THAT IS GOOD INTO MY LIFE THROUGH THE LAW OF ATTRACTION.	I ALWAYS HAVE BAD LUCK. PEOPLE ARE OUT TO GET ME. LIFE IS OUT TO GET ME. I ALWAYS ATTRACT THE NEGATIVE.

FIGURE 10.3

DOMINANT THOUGHTS AND EMOTIONS

ABUNDANCE AND PROSPERITY CONSCIOUSNESS	MENTAL SUBLUXATION
ABUNDANT UNIVERSE	UNIVERSE OF LACK/LIMITATION
DECISIVE	HESITANT
FAIRNESS	PREJUDICE
FAITH	FEAR
FOCUS ON POSITIVES	FOCUS ON NEGATIVES
FULFILLMENT	FRUSTRATION
HOPE	DESPAIR
INNER CALM	INNER TURMOIL
JOY	DEPRESSION
KNOWLEDGE	IGNORANCE
LOVE	HATE
ORDER	CHAOS/CONFUSION
PEACE	ANGER
POSSIBLE	IMPOSSIBLE
PROSPERITY	POVERTY

FIGURE 10.4

Correction of the mental subluxation also means moving an individual into a subconscious state of abundance and prosperity. As we discussed earlier, this consciousness is the belief that we live in an incredibly lavish and abundant universe and that there is plenty of everything to go around; plenty of love, plenty of money, plenty of health, etc. The inexhaustible spirit of the universe never runs empty and is always there waiting for us to bring forth any of our desires. As we begin to make abundance and prosperity consciousness our inner reality, the universe supports us, and it will not be long before our outer world begins to show us exactly that.

However, just like the physical subluxation, chiropractic treatment of the mental subluxation may progress gradually over a short period of time. Many times we are just "faking it until we make it," when it comes to expanding consciousness. The correction of the mental subluxation requires overcoming some fear before an individual's mindset begins to accept this consciousness, especially when it is so foreign to the current mindset of our society. This fear is overcome by the entire process being in total alignment with universal law, and the subtle intuitive prompting of an individual's inner guidance as it reinforces the process to them as being "naturally right."

The ideal result of a mental subluxation correction is a complete state of non-judgment. However, as human beings living in a very complicated society, a complete state of non-judgment can be extremely challenging. After all we have been conditioned to judge virtually everything within our world (see Figure 10.5). If you have any doubt to this statement try a simple experiment: *For the next 24 hours, try to refrain from making any judgments through word, thought or deed about any persons, places, circumstances, objects, money, etc.* I feel if we can start doing this for just ten minutes at a time we have made definite progress!

A WORLD OF JUDGMENT = A WORLD OF DIS-EASE

ARAB	JEW
BLACK	WHITE
BRAND NAME	OFF BRAND
CATHOLIC	PROTESTANT
DEMOCRAT	REPUBLICAN
DESIRABLE	UNDESIRABLE
EXPENSIVE	CHEAP
HANDSOME/PRETTY	UGLY
MEXICAN	ORIENTAL
NICE	MEAN
NOT GUILTY	GUILTY
POLITE	RUDE
RADICAL	CONSERVATIVE
RICH	POOR
RIGHT	WRONG
STYLISH	OUT OF STYLE
THIN	FAT
UPPER CLASS	LOWER CLASS

FIGURE 10.5

Although this is a weak attempt at humor on my part, there is nothing humorous about judging. When we judge anything we automatically "lock up" the spirit of the universe within our bodies. This is extremely detrimental to us, taking years off our lifespan and blocking incredible abundance and prosperity from coming into our lives. Although very difficult, a state of non-judgment should be the ideal for which we strive. Keep in mind that absolute non-judgmental perfection may not be mandatory at this point in our evolution of consciousness. However, by judging less than what we have previously, we will begin to see tremendous results within our lives!

During correction of the mental subluxation we are also assisted by another mechanism. Our faith in the abundance of the universe is continually strengthened as we begin to experiment with a timeless law.

Law of Giving and Receiving

Emerson referred to this law as the law of compensation, and there is no better way of expanding our mindset and permanently ingraining the consciousness of abundance and prosperity within us. Simply stated as the more you give the more you receive, the law of giving and receiving breaks the mental subluxation of limitation and lack by proving to us time and time again that we live in an unlimited abundant universe.

A chiropractor reminds individuals that whatever you would like to receive, all you have to do is give it. If you want more time, give more time. If you want more money, give more money. If you want more love in your life, give more love. The list goes on and on. The point is consistently stressed that if you are lacking in any area of your life, it is because you are a tightwad somewhere! Although we laugh at that, we ultimately find that by starting to practice the law of giving and receiving, the consciousness of abundance and prosperity starts to become ingrained within us.

Catherine Ponder wisely states that there is essentially only one problem in life: congestion. Conversely, she states there is only one solution: circulation. The mental subluxation is congestion and the chiropractor is there to evaluate potential congested areas. Once these areas are determined, the chiropractor supports and encourages the individual to release the self limiting and sabotaging mental subluxations, allowing the spirit of the universe to flow freely again.

Another wonderful realization that individuals commonly come to after working with the law of giving and receiving is this: *WHEN WE GIVE, WE CAN ONLY GIVE TO OURSELVES!*

Although we may share separate identities in the physical and mental plane, our connection to the infinite is shared by every human being on the planet. It is impossible to interact with any other individual on the planet, and not be interacting with ourselves through our interconnectedness. Knowing this, our lives are never the same. We begin to see the spiritual in everybody and everything. I am convinced that if this realization were embraced by our planet, it would single-handedly solve every problem known to man. After a realization of this interconnectedness, we are compelled to make all interactions with others only at a level that is from the highest and most loving aspect of our being.

Notes

Chapter Eleven
<u>Unleashing Your Spiritual Giant Within</u>

"Oh man there is no planet, sun or star could hold you, if you but knew what you are!"
Ralph Waldo Emerson

As purely spiritual beings each human is the most magnificent, the most perfect, the most remarkable and splendid creation in God's universe. However, at this particular point in time, we are also experiencing physical and mental existences. This is why we can sometimes forget our perfection and stay off our remarkable and splendid path. Physical and mental subluxations can be created and block our sprirtual essences. Chiropractic's role is to minimize these subluxations to maximize the expression of the spirit of life.

As we talk of maximizing the spirit within, it is helpful to remember the image of the garden hose with the water pressure turned up to 100%, as it travels above, down, inside and out. This is always the goal of chiropractic regarding the spirit within an individual. 100% maximum expression within that individual's body.

Throughout the pages of this book we have certainly come to know that humanity's truest nature is as spiritual giants. Even though some of us currently may be "sleeping" spiritual giants, nonetheless, we cannot escape this ultimate truth. One of the main purposes of this book, and certainly a vital function of a chiropractor, is to remind individuals of who they really are and provide them with a conscious awareness of this fact as they interact with the persons, places and circumstances of their physical world. Conscious awareness is the necessary first step in any transformation, and if this is the only accomplishment from this book, it has been an extreme success.

The conscious awareness of a universe of abundance and prosperity may feel a little strange at first. It may even feel like you are lying to yourself or becoming delusional. And, unfortunately, you will probably receive virtually no support from our society and perhaps even occasional ridicule. But we are not looking for support from a society who portrays and reinforces our universe as one of lack and limitation, who judges virtually everything within it, who constantly seduces its peoples at an early age by promises of consumerism and who criticizes and condemns the "impractical dreamers" of individuals who open their hearts and listen, and then intuitively follow their dreams.

Yes, holding conscious awareness of abundance and prosperity may be very difficult but......*DO IT ANYWAY! AND KEEP DOING IT UNTIL IT ULTIMATELY BECOMES INGRAINED IN YOUR SUBCONSCIOUS AND BECOMES A PART OF WHO YOU ARE!*

You will soon start seeing your results. Get prepared because success has a way of coming in a hurry after sometimes enduring a "long haul" of plodding along slowly. The universe starts to reward individuals who begin to remember who they are and live their lives as spiritual beings.

However, you will not be the only one who notices. Others will start seeing the change in you as well. Jesus told us, *"You are the light of the world. A city set on a mountain cannot be hidden. Nor do they light a lamp and then put it under a bushel basket; it is set on a lampstand, where it gives light to all in the house. Just so, your light must shine before others, that they may see your good deeds and glorify your heavenly Father"* (Matthew 5:14).

You will become a "light" in your own little corner of the world. Your light will then start to rub off on others as they seek out to see what it is that is working so well for you. And this, ultimately, brings us one step closer to chiropractic's goal of lifting the entire planet to a higher consciousness by allowing humans to experience a maximum expression of the spirit of the universe within them.

This reminds me of a wonderful story I will never forget involving a minister and his small son. As the minister was working hard on the Sunday sermon one night, his son came into the study and kept distracting him from his work. Finally, after the boy continued to distract him for sometime, the father gave his son a map of the world that he tore out of a magazine.

However, before giving him the map, the father tore it into pieces. He then told his son to try to put it back together, hoping it would keep him busy for a long time.

The minister's son returned in record time with the map all pieced back together. The father asked his son, "How did you do that so fast?" The small child replied innocently, "Well, dad, as you were tearing the map out of the magazine, I noticed a man on the reverse side. I decided that if I made the man whole, the world would fall into place and be all right!"

This story personifies the aim of chiropractic, and about affecting the world by making individuals whole again. By removing subluxations one spine at a time, or one nervous system at a time, we are lifting up the entire planet little by little. Currently only 15% of the population utilizes chiropractic; however, it is only a matter of time before the abundance and prosperity consciousness, through a maximum expression of spirit, begins to filter into the remaining 85%.

Jesus expressly told us, *"Do not look here or there, for the kingdom of heaven is within" (Gospel of Thomas saying 3).* The chiropractic philosophy of above, down, inside and out always requires an individual to look within. The answers to all things always lie within us, and our efforts to look externally for answers and seeming fulfillment will always leave us empty and void inside. Additionally, the answers to our health are not to attack some "evil enemy" external to us, such as medicine's fight against the newest bacteria or organism, but to strengthen the spirit of the individual within. Despite societal appearances, absolutely nothing external to us can harm God's most remarkable and splendid creation. Only we can get in our own way through physical and mental subluxations, and chiropractic is there to help.

Our world is a world of tempting external enticements. Whether in the world of health through nutritional regimens, fad diets, prescription drugs or the latest in surgeries, or outside the health arena through the newest and latest of material possessions, the ceaseless pursuit of money, addictive harmful relationships, the trophy job, the all-knowing televangelist, or the latest in fad churches or religions; we certainly have a wide range of choices! But I am not saying that any of these enticements has the potential to be good or bad or that any should or should not be used. That is up to the individual and how they "attach" themselves to these pursuits. I am saying that *true* fulfillment can only lie within ourselves as we are securely connected to our spiritual essence and that essence is maximally expressed within us. Anything less and we experience the empty void at the end of the day.

With this secure connection to our spirit, we are then free to embrace our external world at will. We are meant to enjoy the richness of this lavish universe. A wise teacher once told me, *To embrace everything, but remain attached to nothing.* Nothing could be more true when dealing with our external world!

This book is meant to develop a consciousness about what we are capable of as human beings who live in a universe of abundance and prosperity. It is about all of us having a long way to go, but now having a clear direction and a state that we can all begin to strive for. It is about a choice that we are all free to make, with nobody being right or wrong by the choice that they ultimately make. This book is about us, hopefully making the choice to maximize the potential of our lives more than what we have in the past. It is about remembering who we truly are and then deciding, no matter where we currently are in our life, that we can always choose today to begin anew. This book is about a health profession that is returning the spiritual back into healing and can lead us to where we want to go.

Chiropractic has always been and always will be about empowering the individual to regain their connection to a maximally expressed spirit within. During this period, the chiropractor forms an equal health "partnership" with the individual and acts only as a facilitator as the individual transforms within. This empowering of the individual and the chiropractor's refusal of the need to be elevated to "pedestal status" is extremely hard to find in the remainder of today's health care industry, and is seldom found outside the chiropractic profession. The reason being, with spirituality rightly returned by chiropractic back into health, an equal partnership between doctor and patient is the only alternative and must be present if permanent transformation is to be successful.

As spiritual beings, temporarily experiencing a physical and mental existence, we must be true to who we are and live a life of maximally expressed spirit. If any of the seven areas of our life are not working, this indicates a less than maximum expression of spirit within our nervous systems. This can occur through a physical or a mental subluxation. Through the philosophy of above, down, inside and out, your chiropractor is ready to help you live the lives you were meant to live. These are lives of unlimited abundance and prosperity that a rich and loving Father has wanted us to have since the beginning of time!

References

benShea, Noah. *Jacob the Baker.* New York: Ballantine Books, 1989.

McArthur, Bruce. *Your Life.* Virginia Beach, Virginia: A.R.E. Press, 1993.

Meyer, Marvin and Bloom, Harold. *The Gospel of Thomas: The Hidden Sayings of Jesus.* New York: Harper Collins, 1992.

Millman, Dan. *The Laws of Spirit.* Tiburon, California: H.J. Kramer Inc., 1995.

Ponder, Catherine. *The Dynamic Laws of Prosperity.* Marina del Rey, California: DeVorss and Co., 1997.

Redfield, James. *The Celestine Prophecy.* New York: Warner Books Inc., 1994.

Talbot, Michael. *The Holographic Universe.* New York: Harper Collins, 1991.

The New American Bible. Washington, D.C.: Confraternity of Christian Doctrine, 1970.

Trine, Ralph Waldo. *In Tune With the Infinite.* London: Thorsons, 1995.

Notes

ORDER FORM

Abundance & Prosperity Center
P.O. Box 116774
Carrollton, Texas 75011-6774

Please send _____ copies of **Above, Down, Inside and Out: Unleashing Your Spiritual Giant Within** to:

Name_____
Company_____
Address_____
City_____
State_____ Zip_____
Telephone_____

Payment:
Check included (payable to Abundance & Prosperity Center)

VISA ∂   MASTERCARD ∂
Card Number_____
Expiration Date_____
Cardholder Signature_____

_____ copies @ U.S. $14.95   _____
_____ copies @ International $18.95 _____
                                  Subtotal _____
        8.25% Tax (Texas residents) _____
Shipping:
$2.00 first book/ $1.00 each additional book _____
                                     Total _____

E-mail: DrMichaelNorman@msn.com
Have your VISA or MASTERCARD ready
Fax Orders   (972) 395-3628

Michael J. Norman B.S. , D.C.

Dr. Norman incorporates chiropractic, universal principles and spirituality within his private practice. He regularly speaks to groups and performs workshops in addition to his practice and his writing. The Abundance & Prosperity Center is dedicated to promoting spiritual values and a non-adversarial, non-competitive consciousness for our planet. He lives with his wife and daughter in Carrollton, Texas. If you or your organization would like to contact Dr. Norman to set up an event, offer any comments, or to assist with this effort, please call or write:

Abundance & Prosperity Center
P.O. Box 116774
Carrollton, Texas 75011-6774
E-mail: DrMichaelNorman@msn.com
Fax (972) 395-3628